Gumption

SOUGHT-AFTER COMMON SENSE AND
INTELLECTUAL TRAINING
FOR INQUIRING EMPLOYEES,
MANAGERS AND BUSINESS OWNERS.

By Lisa M. Rose

First printing 2005

ISBN: 0-9767068-0-6

Gumption Training Company, LLC
P.O. Box 17
Monroe, CT 06468

www.Gumptiontraining.com
(866) 945-9985

Attention Corporations, Universities, Colleges and Professional Organizations:
Quantity discounts are available on bulk purchases of this book for educational, gift purposes, or as premiums for increasing magazine subscriptions or renewals. Special books or book excerpts can also be created to fit specific needs.

Serial number: 76592920
Filing Date: 5/19/2004
Register: Principal
Law Office 110
Mark: Got Gumption? ®
Mark Type: Service Mark
Drawing Type: Stylized Words, letters, or numbers
Filing Basis: Sect 1a

Owner: Rose, Lisa M. (United States, individual)

For: Business Motivational Material
INT. Class 041

Permission to reprint excerpts from Emotional Intelligence by Daniel Goleman granted by Bantam Books, 1995.

Typeset Design: Dante Caliandri
Graphic Design: Jane Mahoney

This book has been printed in Caslon Old Style, 11 point type.

Table of Contents

DEDICATION

Gumption is dedicated to my husband, Dr. George Rose, and my two children, Gracie and Jack. Thank you for all of your support and patience. I would also like to acknowledge my mother, Mary Ellen Connolly. She helped to instill in me inspiration, confidence and an above-average work ethic. Thank you, Mom!

I would like to thank Douglas Fink and Dante Caliandri for all of their expertise in editing the book. In addition, I would like to acknowledge Rich Kuepper, Carol Roberto, Colette Pervais, Nancy Casella, Carol Kennedy, Jim McPartland and Robin Bassett for reviewing my rough drafts, giving me constant feedback and supporting what I believe to be needed in the business world. Last but not least, a special "thank you" goes out to Tim McPartland for researching many of the quotes that are dear to my heart and included in the book and to Jane Mahoney for her creative talents with the design of the book cover.

INTRODUCTION

Gumption: 1) common sense, horse sense; 2) enterprise, initiative
(Merriam Webster Dictionary)

The fundamental lessons recorded in *Gumption* are written with the intention to educate, guide and motivate a person to be the best they can be as an employee and/or manager. In other words, it is specifically written for employees and managers to gain "gumption" in the workplace. According to Merriam Webster Dictionary, gumption is defined as "1) common sense, horse sense 2) enterprise and initiative." In addition, gumption in my mind is when an individual instinctively responds positively to a situation on the job without formally being trained to deal with that situation. In essence they use their gumption to produce a positive outcome. When a person possesses gumption, they demonstrate that they have what it takes to succeed on the job by knowing how to professionally and empathetically interact with all types of personalities and situations, whenever possible. Over time they master the art of working, influencing and leading others by using the right decision-making skills to create a positive outcome each and every time.

A heavy emphasis is applied throughout *Gumption* on understanding human behavior, which is the foundation needed to succeed as a competent employee and as an effective manager. In each chapter, both employees and managers will receive a lesson that will be applied to a specific situation that occurs on the job in most industries. Each lesson will demonstrate to the reader how to understand and apply that lesson from both the employee's standpoint and from the manager's standpoint.

These lessons, if understood and accepted, should help to enhance a person's career potential as well as their personal life. It should not be of surprise that some of the lessons found in *Gumption* will remind many readers of human relation skills that they are currently using. Others will read about lessons they have heard or read about from previous training classes, but for one reason or another have chosen not to apply those lessons. For those readers maybe, just maybe, this might be the final time they have to hear the value of the lesson, from a different perspective, to convince themselves of applying the principles behind the lesson. Lastly, for those readers who have never read any type of human relations motivational material, I congratulate you for opening the book and only encourage you to read each chapter with an incessant thirst for knowledge. This is guaranteed to be one of the most influential books of your lifetime. Congratulations ahead of time for having the gumption to read *Gumption*!

The information contained in *Gumption* is based on priceless lessons, advice and training that I have been fortunate enough to obtain, apply and deem to be of value. This communal collection of lessons has been compiled over the years from countless seminars, courses, business books, auto-biographies, workshops, newspapers, magazines, and shared experiences from thousands of people I have interviewed, including human resource professionals, presidents of companies and co-workers. I am hopeful that I can keenly pass these lessons on to others to better prepare them for the business world thereby preventing them from making the same mistakes that others and I have made. In science most inventions are discovered by mistakes being made and this certainly holds true in business, as well. For that reason, I have highlighted many of the most common business situations that occur in all industries and have chosen to share them with the world so that everyone has the opportunity to benefit from these lessons by being a better employee or manager.

In addition to reading each lesson, I highly encourage all employees to review the manager's section and for all managers to review the employee's section since it is intended to teach the other side's perspective.

Surprisingly, many of these fundamental lessons are never found in company-training manuals although they should be. Instead, these essential lessons are usually handed down by great mentors, sometimes over a 20- to 40-year span, and usually only after a mistake has been made on the job. It gives me great pleasure to share this information with all of you, hopefully before the next mistake occurs.

As you journey through life, I encourage you to embrace and learn from your mistakes. After you read this book, I anticipate that you will create a habit of sharing your experiences with others as I have done with you.

A MESSAGE FROM THE AUTHOR

Ever since I can remember I have been enthralled by the difference between motivated, positive people and unmotivated, negative people. It is not just a coincidence that motivated people get promoted and succeed. So what came first, the motivation or the promotion? And what makes a person motivated anyway? Is there a secret character trait that develops in a person to make them motivated or unmotivated? Are they born with it? Is it because of parental influence? A teacher's influence? Genetics? Participation in sports? Life experiences? Where they went to school? The answer is too involved to select just one. What I do know is that it is never too late to get motivated. Sometimes just a book, such as *Gumption*, can deliver the answers and insight needed to help a person realize that they too can accomplish what they want to do in life and be who they aspire to be by just believing in themselves and applying a relentless, persistant focus towards their goals.

BACKGROUND HISTORY

At 20 years of age, while in between college transfers from Keene State to Southern Connecticut State University (SCSU), I read the autobiography of Lee Iacocco (Lido Iacocco). In the first few chapters of the book, he suggested that everyone could benefit from "Dale Carnegie Training", whether they were a businessperson, salesperson or housewife. I figured if this successful businessman from Chrysler Corporation saw the value in "Dale Carnegie Training", then so should I. The following summer I enrolled in a Dale Carnegie class on human relation skills in Woodbridge, CT. The course instruction contained public speaking, negotiation, leadership and conflict resolution material. Most of the students in the class were in their early to late 40's and were required or guided by their employers to take the course. It was during this 14-week course that I witnessed life-changing events.

One of the students in the course, Charlie (name changed), was a grumpy 48-year-old manufacturing manager, set in his ways, not open to change. In just 14 weeks, he emerged into a positive, enthusiastic and open-minded manager. On the final night of the course, "Charlie" personally came up to me and praised me for taking such a powerful course at the beginning of my life and career. Charlie confided in me by saying "I wish I would have enrolled in this class at 20 years of age, instead of waiting until I was almost 50. I would have lived my life completely different and probably would not have divorced my wife, which would have resulted in me not having to raise my children in two separate households." That comment was a major awakening to me, as I realized then, that I had stumbled upon one of the most valuable courses a person could take in their lifetime. I only wished that I had taken the course sooner instead of waiting until I was 20 years old!

For the next year, while attending SCSU pursuing a degree in Biology, I chose to volunteer my time as a graduate assistant for Dale Carnegie Systems. Words cannot describe the value I gained from volunteering my time. It was an absolute thrill to hear and witness lifealtering events that were occurring in each of the student's lives due to the impact of the course content. These events were occurring because the students were learning and implementing basic human behavior principles taught in the Dale Carnegie course. This experience is never-ending.

The Dale Carnegie course played an intregal role in helping me to better understand human behavior in business and in my personal life. This understanding helped me to quickly advance in my career from working my way through college as a waitress/bartender to a sales position in the telecommunications industry. After six months in the industry, I left for a better opportunity as a recruiter with the Monroe Group in Monroe, Connecticut. Within a year and a half, I had advanced from a recruiting position to a management position. After managing the office for 3 years, I then opened another office for the Monroe Group in Norwalk, CT. After building up that office in a year and a half, I was then promoted to a regional manager position managing four offices in Fairfield County, CT. In August of 2004, I initiated and was awarded a multi-million dollar "on-site managed vendor program" with the second largest consumer products manufacturer in the world (for solicitation purposes, I have decided not to include the company name).

I am absolutely certain that the basic principles that I electively learned early on in my career were the primary reasons why I continue to stay motivated and why I advanced in my career so rapidly. It is important for me to mention that it was not just the money I was earning that was making me happy on the job; it was also the principles that I believed in and was able to reinforce on a daily basis with co-workers and clients that made me happy in my job and with myself.

Fortunately, through my recruiting experience, having interviewed literally thousands of people, I have also come to the conclusion that there is not a perfect company, job or industry out there for anyone. Instead it is all what employees make of it that makes the job interesting, rewarding or at least a good stepping-stone towards a better career.

An additional reason why I am sharing these lessons with the world is to help companies reduce their employee turnover ratio by improving their management staff. According to the American Management Association, one of the primary reasons employees leave their jobs is because of poor management. Now, I don't think there is a manager out there today who intentionally becomes a poor or incompetent manager. Instead, he or she usually is promoted to a position of management because they were a high performer and the natural reaction for most companies when they have high performers is to keep promoting them to keep them satisfied. Unfortunately, there is a negative consequence to promoting the best performers. The fact is many highproducing employees do not make good managers. It does not mean they cannot learn to be a good manager; it is just that many are promoted into the role without the proper tools to lead, understand human behavior and/or motivate correctly at that time. Can you think of a high performer that you worked for who was not good at leading others?

Being promoted to a manager is similar to parenthood. Most parents have never taken a class in childhood education, yet they chose to have children. They rely instead on their own instincts and sometimes they listen to the advice of others. Most of the time their instincts were right but in hindsight they might have done something slightly different, if only they had known better. Does this sound familiar from a management perspective? The same applies to newly promoted managers with no formal management training. *Gumption* is intended to give employees and managers the hindsight before problems occur so that they can manage themselves and others effectively when the situations arise.

HOW TO GET THE MOST
OUT OF EACH LESSON

Each chapter contains a lesson that is introduced. At the end of the lesson, there is a message to "Employees" on how to best use the lesson in business and/or with their co-workers and managers. I then have a suggestion to "Managers" on how to best use the lesson with their own employees and/or co-workers. I once again encourage everyone to read both "Employees" and "Managers" material because it will teach the other side's perspective.

Throughout the book there are also a few valuable "Life Lessons" that taught me early on about people and human relations. I encourage everyone to read this book several times throughout their lifetime because many of the chapters will not relate to the reader at that moment. However, as the reader grows and matures they will eventually be faced with similar situations and can refer to the book as a guide. The following quote helps to reinforce this statement. "The teacher will arrive when the student is ready." (unknown)

According to a recent Gallup poll, an average of 15-20% of employees in many Fortune 500 companies, have the potential to be fired because they are unproductive or incompetent. This survey was conducted amongst many of today's top leading CEO's. Does this come as a surprise? Is it an accurate reflection of the company that you are working for? Should 15-20% of the staff employed at your present company be let go or replaced? Let's just assume for a moment that the poll is correct, and that an average of 20% of every company's staff should be let go or replaced for not meeting the company's expectations. What do you suppose could be causing an average of 20% of employees to be incompetent? Could it be that they are having personal issues at home, health problems or worklife balance difficulties? Maybe they are lacking in training and guidance from immediate management? Some might be experiencing personal issues with their current manager or a co-worker, while others have simply lost interest and motivation on the job. Lastly, some of the employees could have finally been promoted to a position of incompetence in which they now lack the technical or management skills to perform their job well.

Can you identify the employees in your company that should be let go for poor performance? For those employees that you identified, could they be more successful if they just stopped doing one thing that they are doing wrong? Is it something that is easy to correct or are there just too many faults to correct? I would like to confidently guess that most of the reasons that you identified why those certain employees can be let go are not technically related at all, but are instead related to how they deal and interact with other people. Is this true?

So what do these 20% have to do to save their job? Simply stated, they need to follow the suggestions in this book. At any given time you personally may be exposed to one of the reasons above that could cause you to slip into the 20%, if you do not respond positively to the condition. No one is safe! At any given time you may be the person who: has a horrible boss that does not give direction well; is asked to work with a co-worker who is lazy and incompetent; or start to have health problems that may affect your job performance. How people react to these challenging situations is what differentiates them from being in the 80% range of performing well enough on the job or in the 20% range of being in jeopardy of losing their job.

I have listened to and applied the advice from many successful business people over the years. The "secrets to success principles" most of the business leaders preach year after year are easy to follow, but unfortunately a good percentage of the business population does not think those principles could, would or should apply to them. They either believe that the common well-known principles don't work or that they just don't need to apply them to their daily tasks or routine. Well, I hope this has been your wake-up call to realize that 20% of you better change your behavior towards working with others or you will quickly be replaced.

The fact is these principles do work and all it takes is a little bit of discipline when it comes to applying them to the daily tasks and eventually they will become second nature.

Lesson 1

"The majority of things that
people stress out about never happen."
— Dale Carnegie

THINK ABOUT THIS, when was the last time you stressed out about something? Did it actually happen? The statistics state, probably not. Did you recently have a client that threatened to stop doing business with you? Meanwhile, you stressed out for an entire day thinking the worst only to find out it was a waste of energy and time to stress out over it. The best advice someone gave me years ago was that "99% of the things that people stress out about never happen."

In the sales office of any company in any industry, this 99% rule should be enforced. If the sales office has at least two sales representatives calling on potential clients, then there will eventually be a time when one of the sales representatives will call on a potential client of the other sales representative's list of prospective clients. The tension will heighten between both employees until a compromise is agreed upon. The unfortunate consequence is that 99% of the time the stress that was created between the two employees could have been prevented, had the employees understood that more than 99% of the situations they stressed out about never came to fruition. This is such an emotionally charged subject that it needs to be repeated. In business, there are many times when employees, in general, will get upset because someone has intruded on their potential business or their job duties. The employees involved will argue or ignore each other for a period of time until a compromise is agreed upon and then they will realize that they have wasted their effort over nothing because the client never chose to do business with the company in the first place. Please remember this rule so that, as an employee or manager, you will respond to situations correctly and will know which situations you should not give any attention to. *Don't stress out over things that haven't happened; it is very unproductive.*

EMPLOYEES:

If you really are in sales, I guarantee there will eventually be a time when a co-worker of yours will call on one of your potential clients and it will cause you to temporarily resent that co-worker. Before you go to your manager or another employee to complain about the co-worker, evaluate the situation. Did he/she successfully get an appointment with the client? If the answer is yes, then sit down and talk about a strategy that could work to bring the prospective client into the company. Maybe that sales representative called a completely different person within the company that you never knew about; then you could both agree to keep individually calling on the company. If the answer is "no" that an appointment wasn't set up with the company, then communicate with the co-worker and come to a mutual agreement as to who is going to call on the client going forward. The employee with the best relationship with the client and the employee that can successfully get the business should be the one calling on the client. If neither of you have worked with the client, then set a deadline as to how long the first sales representative should continue calling on the client before it should be passed on to another employee.

Hint: According to Dale Carnegie people will do business with people that remind them of themselves or that they have something in common with. In addition, people will hire people that remind them of themselves. When making a sales call, look for commonality and similarities. The employee that builds the best relationship to gain the business should be the person calling on the account and that is usually the person that has the most things in common with the client. The point I want you to understand is that many employees "stress out" about potential events on the job that never actually come to fruition. This unproductive stress only wastes time and energy and reduces employee moral which breaks down cooperation between employees. Make sure if you are to call on an account, that you check on the account status in the database or communicate with the manager to see if anyone is already calling on the account and investigate what the activity/history level has been. Going forward, don't stress out over something that has not happened.

MANAGERS:

When an employee comes to you upset because another employee has "called" on one of their potential accounts, let them vent, listen to all of the facts and wait for them to calm down. Evaluate the account status by looking for correct documentation in the computer that should be noted on the previous sales calls. Enforce with your employees that they must document every call or visit. Check to see if the current employee has brought in any business with the account. How long has the current employee been calling on the account? Are they speaking to the right person? As a manager, please make sure that your employees know how to qualify the right person or persons that have the decision-making power to grant your company the right to do business with them. When you initially train your new employees, make sure they know the steps that are used to evaluate an account. When two employees are upset about an account that is currently not doing business with the company, first make them realize that they are upset about something that might not even happen. Tell them to follow the guidelines that you have set up in the office. If you, as a manager, feel a different employee should call on the account because they have a better relationship with the client, make the change. Tell them also to take the emotion out of the situation because it is just business. Once again, these steps will slowly teach your own employees to realize that 99% of the situations that they get upset about never happen.

Lesson 2

Back to the basics.

IT'S A WELL-KNOWN FACT that the busier an employee gets on the job, the easier it can be for them to forget about the basics. This classically happens in business and sports. In the speed of business or in sports "the game" starts to advance so quickly when the pace picks up. Eventually, confidence starts to increase, egos start to emerge and wham, someone skips a basic step or task and the game or the account is lost. There is an understood rule that has been handed down from generation to generation and that is to be aware that professional football and baseball players became professionals *because they mastered the basics*. A professional team is not capable of mastering advanced plays without mastering the basics first. Professional athletes don't take the basics for granted either. Instead, they practice them over and over so that they become inherent.

This basics breakdown usually occurs in business with a complaint from a client. Here are a few examples of mastering the basics in business.

In the restaurant industry, food quality and cleanliness are the basics that have to be mastered. The standards for food quality are enforced by following routine instructions on food storage, prep and cooking instructions. Cleanliness is enforced by teaching the staff how to keep a restaurant clean by using unique tactics such as "never enter the kitchen without something in your hands, which helps to keep the dining area clutterfree" and "always wash your hands when leaving the bathroom."

In the construction industry, the basic rule of thumb that carpenters learn early on to "measure twice and cut once." This helps to ensure that carpenters have the correct dimensions before they start the job.

In the staffing industry, after all of the initial interviews take place to fill a specific position and an employee is about to receive an offer, human resources will be busy performing their pre-employment screenings on the candidate to ensure they are hiring a candidate that will pass their requirements. The pre-employment screening could involve several of the following:

previous job references, salary history confirmations, credit checks, drug tests, personality profile tests, criminal background checks, driving record investigations, etc. Any one of these screening measures can legally be used to identify a person that should not be hired into the company. They are purposely enforced to disqualify candidates that could create problems in the workforce. If the company requires a drug, criminal, reference checks and a social security check before employment, then every one of these checks should be done before the employee starts working on the job. When just one of these checks is overlooked or not investigated, and the wrong candidate is placed into the company, uncomfortable situations can occur that could have been prevented had the basic steps not been forgotten about or overlooked. An example would be hiring a school bus driver without doing one of the following: a drug test, driving record investigation, reference checks or criminal background check. To overlook just one of those checks on a potential candidate could be disastrous! Just remember, there are many people that are great actors during an interview. Don't just go on gut, check them out. Your job could depend on it! Peoples lives could depend on it!

In the sales industry, business developers learn early on to qualify their prospects in order to make sure their time is not wasted on non-decision makers. If the basics are skipped by not qualifying a lead, then weeks and sometimes months or years can be lost by chasing a dead-end prospect. Meanwhile, all the business developer had to do was qualify the candidate by asking "are you the right person to talk to in reference to _____?" In business, don't skip the basics by not qualifying prospects.

EMPLOYEES:

The basics in business also consist of doing the common courtesy tasks such as: returning all phone calls and e-mails in a timely manner and sending out thank you cards to any new client that you spend at least 15 minutes with during the day. Many high producers who are considered successful in their industry are often interviewed and the classic response to the secret to their success is that they made sure they never forgot to do the basics. In fact, they considered themselves to be true professionals at the basics. These high producers became successful in what they do because they never forgot to complete the simple tasks. Ironically, the not-so-successful people in the same industry usually don't think the basics apply to them, such as, returning all voice-mails, e-mails or sending thank you cards. How do these employees expect to build on their foundation if they haven't mastered the basics? To become a successful worker in your industry, make a commitment to never overlook the basics and the rewards will be tenfold.

MANAGERS:

It is inevitable that every six months or so you will probably have to take care of a situation that was caused by an employee who overlooked a basic task. It is wise to set up reminders of what the expectations are that the employees need to follow to consistently deliver the service that the customer is expecting. In example, let's look at an overnight delivery company that guarantees next day delivery by 10 AM every business morning. If that company is going to meet its advertised promise to the customer, then that company needs to ensure that every employee who works for their company is aware of the promise and knows what they need to do to deliver on that promise to the customer each and every time.

As a leader, show the employees what has to be done to make sure that the basics are being performed. Create a checklist if you have to, to make sure all the procedures are being performed for every order of business that occurs in your office. Take this seriously because most often business is not lost because of a technical reason. It is usually lost because someone dropped the ball and did not follow through with what they had promised to do. Also, be aware that mistakes are going to happen. Try to minimize the amount of errors that will occur by constantly reinforcing the basics. Again, checklists are great.

Think about the last client your company just signed on. Did that company sign on because their last vendor (your competitor) dropped the ball? That ball probably had something to do with forgetting to do a basic task. Always reinforce with yourself and the staff that the basics cannot be overlooked and make them aware of the consequences. As a manager, be active in each account that is under your control, or at least delegate to someone in the company to make quality control calls to each and every client on a monthly basis to ensure that the company is servicing the client up to their expectations and to also see if any other needs might be serviced.

Lesson 3

Internal communication with managers and co-workers is the lifeline of a business.

COMMUNICATION IS ESSENTIAL in any type of relationship, business being no exception. Internal communication with co-workers and managers is the lifeline. Without it, production, employee morale and company credibility dies. Have you ever made a call to a vendor and the vendor does not return the call? Have you ever worked with a contractor to make changes to your house and the contractor starts the project but then disappears for days without returning any of your calls? Or better yet, when an employee does not show up to work, instead of calling to say they are out because of a death in the family or because of an illness, they choose not to call and not to show up for work! All of these examples cause the people that are affected by the lack of communication to question the person at fault and the consideration of ending the relationship between the two parties arises all because of a *lack of communication.*

EMPLOYEES:

Make a point of never leaving your office without a list of phone numbers to call in case you run late to a meeting with a client or manager. It is critical to always call ahead and apologize if you do run late to show the person that you respect their time. Even if you are running late to your own job, call ahead to communicate with your co-workers and managers to let them know what time you will arrive so that others are not inconvenienced. This helps to reduce a lot of anxiety that is built up in the office wondering where you are. Another important example of establishing clear internal communication is when a new policy or procedure is implemented but the introduction is vague or unclear. As an enforcer of the new policy or procedure it is critical that you do not proceed with the new change until you understand the new policy fully. Take the time to ask questions. Don't let a minute go by because the consequences can be disastrous. One of the worst things an employee can do is to accept new information that is unclear to them. The result will be that they will follow the guidelines or present that new unclear information to clients without really understanding the contents of the information. This will result in a reduction in the company's credibility since the person representing the company is not trained properly because they don't understand their own material. Make sure as an employee that you understand your material first before you try to represent the company. Ask questions when something is unclear to increase your own knowledge, save face and keep the company credibility high.

MANAGERS:

In reference to communicate, a good habit to get into is to hold weekly meetings with each of your staff members. These meetings will allow you, as a manager, to eliminate any confusion about company expectations, new material, policies, procedures or ethics training. It also allows the manager to coach or mentor the employee and even go over any basic training that the employee might need to review.

Often times when an employee has been identified as not performing to company expectations, one of the reasons is because they did not absorb the initial new hire training material properly. As a manager, once an employee has been identified as "not fully performing to company expectations" it is mandatory to set up a one-to-one meeting. In this meeting, the manager must identify the areas that need improvement and the manager has to ask the employee why they are having difficulty. More often than not the real reason will come out and the solution is usually something that can be solved by additional training. A good example of this is when an employee is identified as not meeting company expectations because they do not fully understand how to utilize the company software. Instead of the employee going to a manager and asking for additional training, they will instead remain silent and just try to perform their job without using the software or by using the software on an entry level basis.

These one-to-one communication meetings will also allow a manager to get a pulse on what is going on with each individual employee. If the manager cannot personally conduct these meetings, then they should delegate the task to a supervisor or another manager or try to conduct the meetings once a quarter with each employee if possible.

The last resort for managers who cannot find the time to attend the one-to-one meetings is to implement a conference call or e-mail broadcast so that all of the employees who don't get a chance to sit down with their managers on a regular basis can at least have an idea as to what the company's current financial status, changes in policies, philosophy, strategy, mission and goals are for the current year and years to come.

In conclusion, internal communication is essential for business to run smoothly. Invest in your employees by scheduling regular meetings with your staff to keep everyone informed and properly trained. When new policies and procedures are introduced, make sure everyone is well informed as to why the policy is in effect, how it affects each employee personally and how the policy is followed. Always have an open door policy for employees to come to managers to clarify any misunderstandings and to give suggestions as to how to improve processes and procedures. The end result of investing in proper training of new procedures and enforcing weekly, monthly or quarterly one-to-one meetings with employees will be an increase in more competent employees, higher employee productivity, sound company credibility and increased morale.

Lesson 4

*Always take the approach to understand
the situation from both sides.*

To UNDERSTAND A SITUATION from both sides, imagine you are driving on the road and a person cuts you off. Your knee-jerk reaction is to immediately get defensive and probably say a profanity or two. However, the driver that cut you off is probably unaware of your outrage until they hear you blare your horn and let them have it. In this situation, you have automatically assumed it was their fault and that he or she is just a crazy lunatic on the streets. Does this sound familiar? What you haven't considered is this question: could you have been at fault? If that answer is absolutely not, then consider these questions:

- If it was their fault, then why did they do it?
- Was there a chance that maybe they were rushing a person to the hospital with a serious injury?
- Maybe they were upset because a loved one has just been injured and because of that they were not paying attention to their driving responsibility.
- Maybe they are senior citizens who just came from the ophthalmologist after being diagnosed with cataracts and are now legally blind but are still driving until they agree to have cataract surgery to bring their vision back to 20/20. (For your information this happens more often than you think!)

While certainly not advocating for reckless drivers to be allowed to cut people off on the road, these examples should cause good drivers to consider that maybe the reckless driver's situation might just be worse off than their own. So in those cases, when a near miss situation does arise, the good driver should just remain calm and be grateful for two reasons. First, they must be grateful that a car accident did not occur. Secondly, they should be grateful that they are not in the reckless driver's "shoes" or have the problems that the reckless driver has at that moment. This perspective works well in conflict situations on the job as well. The next time you have a person who is rude to you, evaluate their situation and try to understand what pressures they might be under. *Try at that point to be grateful you are not in their shoes.*

EMPLOYEES:

The next time you are on the road and a person cuts you off, instead of reacting by losing your temper or speeding up to nudge their bumper, try to evaluate what they might be going through and the problems that they probably have. *Think long and hard if there is anything that makes you want to be them and then just be glad you are not them.* This is a much better way of dealing with a bad driver than road rage.

In addition, the next time a person is rude to you on the job, evaluate that person and realize that at any given time in your life you probably wouldn't want to walk in their shoes. *Be grateful that you are not that person and just move on.*

MANAGERS:

It is crucial to use this "understanding both sides approach" at all times. When at all possible, get both sides of the story before a decision is made. Many times, problems will arise between co-workers. As a manager, it is highly suggested to stay neutral to both parties and let both parties know that a decision will be based solely on the facts presented and that all emotion will be removed from the situation. Managers are to be especially careful not to react or give opinion to either party involved or to talk to one party about the other party.

> *"A little bit of experience often upsets a whole lot of theory."*
> — Cadmen

> *"Unjust criticism is often a disguised compliment."*
> — Dale Carnegie

According to Daniel Goleman, author of *"Emotional Intelligence"* (copyright 1995, Bartan Books, pg. 36)

"Much evidence testifies that people who are emotionally adept who know and manage their own feelings well and who read and deal effectively with other peoples feelings are at an advantage in any domain of life, whether romance and intimate relationships or picking up the unspoken rules that govern success in organizational politics. People with well developed emotional skills are also more likely to be content and effective in their lives, mastering the habits of mind that foster their own productivity; people who cannot marshal some control over their emotional life fight inner battles that sabotage their ability for focused work and clear thought."

Lesson 5

"Everyone loves to talk about themselves."
— Dale Carnegie

ACCORDING TO DALE CARNEGIE, the most effective way to get a person to like you is to allow that person to talk about himself or herself. Try to exercise this well-known human relations principle at the next networking event that you attend. Introduce yourself to a stranger by asking them their name. Allow that person to talk only about themselves by asking questions that relate to them, not you. Caution: please do not sabotage your first impression by asking questions that are too personal; this would cause the stranger to conclude their first impression of you as being too nosey or inquisitive. Instead, keep the conversation light but focused on them. By the end of the conversation, the person who just spoke about themself will have developed a liking to you simply because you allowed them to talk about the most important person in the world, who is themself.

Another way to apply this famous principle is in the dating scene. If you are dating a person and you want to make the person like you more, simply ask them questions that allow them to talk about themselves and listen to what they have to say. Once again, they will walk away from the date realizing they liked talking to you because you allowed them to talk about themselves. The important step with both of these examples is to actually remember what the person's answers are to the questions you asked them. It is amazing how many people lack good listening skills. Try to stand apart from millions of people in the world today by paying attention to the important details of a person's life. The extra effort of asking, listening and remembering personal information of your clients and friends will reward you financially, spiritually and socially.

Often voted one of most stressful tasks for business people is the awkward initial introduction either on the phone or in person. This is often referred to as a cold call. The best advice that I have heard and accepted from many of the world's best business trainers would be to separate the steps of the introduction into two categories. The first category applies to a face-to-face introduction. The second category applies to a phone introduction.

(Face to Face):

- Put a smile on your face.
- Make eye contact.
- Listen to their tone of voice and adapt to their speed of speech to communicate at the same pace. Earlier I had mentioned that people like to do business with people that remind them of themselves. Well, it is not any different when it comes to speaking with someone. If you are speaking with someone who is a slower talker than you then quickly slow down the pace so that they will like you more because you speak like them. If you are speaking to a fast talker, then try to speed up your pace to make them relate better while speaking to you. Exercise this principle the next time you meet a person for the first time.
- Quickly develop a rapport with the person to gain a common interest.
- Qualify if they may be a person you prefer to do business with.
- Don't complain about anything, stay positive.

(Over the Phone):

- Put a smile on your face. Everyone can feel a smile through the phone. (No one wants to talk to someone with a frown on their face except for maybe another person with a frown on their face.)
- Listen to their tone of voice and adapt to their speed of speech to communicate at the same pace.
- Make sure you have the right person on the phone by qualifying them with a question like, "are you the right person that makes the decisions about the company insurance policy?"
- Once you qualify the prospect, quickly develop a rapport with the person to gain a common interest.
- Don't complain about anything, stay positive.

EMPLOYEES:

As an employee of a company, it is usually imperative to get to know your co-workers as quickly as possible, especially the co-workers who can contribute to your overall success on the job. If your goal is to make the best impression possible, then upon each introduction with a new co-worker, follow the suggested guidelines:

- Smile and introduce yourself.
- Remember the co-workers name and say it correctly.
- Ask them something that will make them talk about themselves. (for example, how long have you been with the company? What department are you in?)
- Listen to how they talk and speak at their pace.
- If you notice that they have a picture on their desk of their family, ask how old their kids are and keep a mental note of the children's names. The next time you see that person, remember to ask them how their children are by name. You will be pleasantly surprised to see how shocked they are that you actually remembered their children's names.
- Make a habit of always saying good morning and good evening to every person that you walk by each and everyday. If the group is too large, always make a point of saying "Good morning, everyone" or "Good night everyone".
- Don't complain a lot. People tend to ignore employees who complain too much. Stay positive.

MANAGERS:

Don't assume your employees know how to effectively communicate at functions and during client networking events. Train your employees on the importance of making a great first impression. Enforce with your employees that a client will only do business with a person they are comfortable with and someone they can relate to and trust. Always supply your employees with new human relation tools that will constantly enhance their understanding of human behavior. As a manager, it is your responsibility to attend business calls with your staff to observe their people skills with clients. It is frightening to witness a business call when an untrained, egotistical business person dominates the conversation, bores the clients and kills the business deal because of it. For example, many unbeknownst self-centered or egotistical "business professionals" will take a client out to lunch or dinner to help seal a business deal. In horror, the entire relationship can be ruined if a self-centered business professional talks about himself the entire time, instead of allowing the client to talk about them self. The irony of the unconscious self-centeredness is that most often the person talking about himself, believes he is a great conversationalist and that he is just doing his job keeping the conversation flowing and entertaining his client. (How unfortunate.)

As a manager, it is your duty to make sure your employees are not annoying clients and killing business relationships. Coach your employees to always pay attention to their client's interests, not their own. *Don't assume your employees know this skill.* Make sure that you have each employee attend a lunch or dinner meeting with you and a client, to witness the correct way to entertain a client.

Life Lesson #1

Don't rely on a company to promote you; instead get yourself promoted and choose wisely who you work for.

I RECENTLY ATTENDED A performance workshop in October of 2004, in Stamford, CT. The workshop was led by a team of consultants that were discussing how companies could improve their employees performance levels by adopting the training programs of other successful companies, such as: incentifying individual producers differently based on performance, stock option plans, increasing bonus structures, developing quicker career advancement opportunities, increasing company training, etc. Although the information that was discussed and debated was certainly of value, I walked away from that workshop with the same belief that I walked in with, which is employees should not rely on other companies to advance them in their career. Instead, employees need to rely on themselves to perform better, not a company career action plan since that could take years to get noticed, and no job is guaranteed these days!

The shear investment that you are doing right this moment by reading *Gumption* will launch your career more than any performance guideline. Why? Because although performance programs are highly needed and work well for many people, they do not work well for everyone. Ironically, at the end of the meeting, after many ideas were proposed, the overall agreement was that it is hard to change employees bad habits, that incentive plans don't work for everyone and that everyone is still looking for the answer as how to improve employee performance! *Here is the answer: the employee has to invest in themselves.* They have to start not on the first level in the company but actually on the bottom basis level and work their way to the first level. The only way they can do that is by passing the basic training requirements of knowing how to interact with people; knowing how to communicate effectively; knowing how to share ideas; knowing what is acceptable, and not acceptable to say to people; what is the right way to listen to someone, etc.

The point I am making here is many people are missing out on getting promoted not because they don't have the technical skills to do the job, it is because they have not mastered their soft skills or their basic skills that they need to be promoted. So how does this get accomplished? Well, if companies could afford it, they should send every employee through basic training, not on what the company does but on the basics of professional interaction, communication, stress management, etc. This would develop more people in a shorter amount of time in comparison to what companies have spent years trying to accomplish to no avail. Think about a manager's daily "to do list", how many of those tasks are employee relations related? About 20-50%? Wouldn't it be nice to reduce that down to 5%-10% by effectively training those employees ahead of time so that the manager could focus on his job better? Preventative maintenance; train the new employees ahead of time with the basics. (This is why I wrote *Gumption.*)

It is a fact that not every company has the best performance metrics in place and even the best companies that think they have it all together are questioning if they are getting the best output of all of their staff. Even the best run companies, such as Pitney Bowes and GE, attend these meetings to find out what is new in the marketplace because they too have people that are not satisfied on the job or are unmotivated. They too, have incentive plans that don't work for everyone. So why do I tell you about this lesson? It is to make a point that you should *not* rely on a company to make you successful. Instead, rely on yourself, invest in yourself. Get yourself promoted because you are the best at what you do, not because you fulfilled your 3-year stay as a manager and now it is time to switch to a different job so that you don't become stale. Don't wait that long. Keep improving yourself by taking on new responsibilities and the promotions will happen sooner than later.

The next decision is to decide who do you base your career with? When selecting a company to work for, there are several questions that should be asked. An employee should never be too quick to accept an offer of employment. As a company policy, human resource departments research references on employees before they make an offer of employment. It is just as fair that an employee should research a company to ensure that their career does not get diverted unexpectedly by choosing to work for a company that is going out of business or has a poor reputation in the industry. The following are a list of suggested questions that employees and managers should use to qualify a prospective company before accepting an offer of employment. These questions are intended to bring to the table any red flags that might indicate to the potential new hire not to take the position. Please note: these are only suggestions that are intended to help an employee make a qualified decision once an offer has been given. *Do not ask these questions during the first interview.*

Pre-Employment Company Reference Steps:

1) Potential employees should conduct research on the prospective company by visiting the company's website and other competitor's websites for any up-to-date changes taking place at the current company or in the industry that can alert the potential employee of legal or financial situations that the company/industry could be suffering from. Financial news sites can also provide helpful information.

2) They should make sure they understand and believe in the products that the company manufacturers/delivers/services.

3) Is the industry that the company is in stable? Have a credit check done on the company. Is the company on the market to be sold? Employees should be cautious not to jump too quickly by quitting a stable job before they research to see if the potential company might be sold, which would result in a layoff.

4) Is the company planning on relocating?

5) How well funded is the company?

6) Does the company pay out on quarterly or annual bonuses? How often have they met the corporate goals to pay out the bonuses?

7) What type of benefits (medical, dental, insurance, life, disability, etc.) does the company provide and how much is the contribution monthly? Is there a matching 401K plan? Stock options?

8) What is the salary potential of the current position that is being considered?

9) Is the environment safe where the company is located? Are there any health hazards to the job? Does the company provide protective equipment?

10) Are there any class action lawsuits that could jeopardize the stability of the company/industry?

11) Does the company have the product in stock when a client wants to order? If not, how long does it take to make the product?

12) How supportive is the customer service department in the company? Is there a customer service department?

13) What is the reputation of the company in the local area?

14) What is the turnover rate of employees? (Turnover rate is how often employees quit or get fired. The human resources department will know this number.)

15) Potential employees should research why past employees have left the company in the past few years. Where did they go? Why?

16) What is the management style of the company? What is the organizational structure of the company?

17) What is involved in the training process for new employees and managers? How long is the training?

18) Is there a Human Resources department in the company?

19) Does the job require commuting a far distance or overnight travel? Does this fit into your lifestyle and work life balance?

20) What are the working hours of the job? Are weekends required? Is there mandatory overtime? How often does that happen? Is being on-call required?

21) Does the company have any long-term strategic plans?

22) Do the current employees look happy on the job? What is the office culture like? Is there a positive vibe in the office or does everyone look miserable?

23) Does the company support part time or job sharing?

24) Has the company been recognized for any outstanding achievements or accomplishments?

25) What are the company values, mission statements or corporate governance? Do they mirror your values? Do you agree with them, could you work under their expectations?

26) What type of tests do you have to pass to get hired? Drug test, criminal background? Credit check?

Potential employees can inquire during the initial interview process about the career advancement opportunities that are available to all employees. It is okay to inquire as to what the duration period is that an employee has to wait before they can be considered for promotion or to post out to another department. Timing is critical with this question though because if they ask *that* question too soon, it will tell the interviewer that the candidate is only interested in using the position as a stepping stone. If the interviewer misconstrues the question, it could jeopardize the candidate's chances of receiving an offer.

All of these questions apply to both employees and managers and can be used as decision-making criteria to either accept or decline offers of employment. Because the consequences of changing jobs and careers is so vital to a person's financial well being, it is critical that employees should be on alert at all times for red flags during the interviewing process that might help to prevent them from making the mistake of accepting the wrong job with the wrong company. Here are a few such examples that should be taken seriously.

- Hearing rumors that the company might be sold or relocated.
- Hearing rumors that the company treats their employees badly.
- Hearing rumors that the company has a class action lawsuit against them.
- Hearing rumors that the company is about to outsource the department you are interviewing with at the time.

Potential employees are highly encouraged to conduct the research that is suggested in this lesson so their career stays on the right path and does not get diverted by making an impulse decision to make a move to another company. The consequences of not conducting solid research on potential employers/companies could reduce an employee's hiring potential down the road with future employers. Other areas that could be affected when employees make the wrong move is to establish bad credit problems because they get laid off unexpectedly from a company they thought was stable. The effects of choosing the wrong job or company can also weaken an employee's confidence, morale and attitude. One should be aware that changes at work also affect the family with increased stress and tension at home. These are just a few examples to remind everyone of the risks that are involved in every career change.

By applying selected questions from the list above that are relevant to each employee's needs and by conducting the research and looking for the red flags on companies before accepting the offer of employment, employees should at least minimize the risk involved in making a career change to keep their career on the fast track.

Employees should also remember not to solely rely on a career performance chart to promote them. They should instead take it upon themselves to be the best that they can be in their industry. They should work hard to get noticed and to advance because they earned it not because it is what has been mapped out for them. This is not to say that you shouldn't use the company's performance chart as a guide; instead you should challenge yourself to receive that promotion sooner than later because you out performed everyone else. Keep investing in yourself, don't wait for companies to promote you when they are ready, earn it and make it happen sooner when possible. Work hard, don't be lazy, work well with others, understand people from their perspective, don't complain, listen to helpful advice, find a mentor, believe in yourself, attend any training you can and continue to defy the odds. Once you get that promotion, don't forget how you got there, keep doing everything that you did to get there and keep investing in yourself to build upon your talents and abilities!

Lesson 6

*Do one task at a time and
give each task 100% of your attention.*

I N THE FALL OF 2000, I was managing an office of four employees in Monroe, Connecticut. Earlier that year I had convinced my boss to open another office 25 miles away in Stamford, CT. We had both agreed that I would split my work week in half, spending 2½ days in Monroe and 2½ days in Stamford. I followed my traditional managing responsibilities in each office which consisted of managing the internal staff, interviewing candidates, prospecting and opening up new business, filling jobs and putting "fires out" when they occurred. Within the first 6 months, mistakes started to happen because this lesson had not yet been learned of "doing one task at a time and focusing 100% attention to that task."

On a daily basis, when I would be in the Stamford office, phone calls would come in that were relevant to the Monroe office and vice versa. Because of the interruptions, when I would be recruiting for one office I would be thinking of other positions that also had to be filled in the other office. The end result was that I was not giving any one of my tasks 100% of my effort. My concentration level on each task was probably as low as 40-65%!

After 9 months of constantly trying to play catch-up and on only giving each task an average of 50% or less effort, I mutually agreed with my boss to concentrate on the new office in Stamford, and to promote another employee to manage the already established office in Monroe. It was the right decision to make. The best lesson I learned from this experience is to make *sure that each task that you do is completed with 100% of your attention,* to ensure that the quality of your service is your best effort each and every time.

EMPLOYEES:

When given a task, concentrate solely on one task at a time until that task is completed with your best effort given. Shut your door if you have to, hold all calls, do what it takes to make sure that you are giving that task

100% of your effort. Joy Baldridge, of Baldridge Seminars, a training consultant from Stamford, Connecticut, introduced our company to the concept of "Phone Zone®". She suggested dedicating time out of each week to "Phone Zone Calls". These chunks of time were set up to do just one task repeatedly and in our case it was sales calls. All of the employees were instructed to literally put up a sign in each of their offices that would read "Phone Zone, do not disturb." Joy stated that by doing this, it would allow each employee to focus 100% on their sales calls without being disturbed. While they were in phone zone they were instructed to have all incoming phone calls go into voicemail. By implementing phone zone, it helped our employees to understand the concept of time management, doing like things together, focusing on one task at a time and giving each task 100% effort. Now that was impressive.

Because each business is unique, this one suggestion of phone zone might not relate best for your business. Hopefully, you can use the same "zone" concept to increase productivity or quality. The important point here is to be aware that your quality output will suffer if you don't give each task 100% focus. When we combine similar tasks together we focus better on those tasks. For those of you in sales, you know that your last sales call of the day is usually your best one. This is true because your first call is usually cold and rusty but as you plow through your prospect list you start to get warmed up, your nervousness decreases and your best effort gets delivered at the end because you are confident, experienced and focused.

Another way to implement this lesson is from a listening perspective. The next time you are in a meeting at work with other employees in attendance, make sure that you pay attention 100% by taking notes. (Always make it a habit to be prepared with a pad of paper and a pen at any type of meeting.) Don't expect to memorize everything without taking notes because you will just be setting yourself up for failure. Listen attentively. Keep good eye contact with the speaker. Don't interrupt the speaker. Don't be the person making the wisecrack. If you have a question during a presentation, wait until the speaker is finished talking because most of the time the question will be answered during the speaker's presentation, if you paid 100% attention. Focus on the information by not thinking about any other order of business except for what is being discussed.

In reality this lesson is abused everyday, sometimes every hour, when employees don't focus 100% to each and every conversation they have with co-workers, managers or clients. Typically you might find yourself involved in a conversation while multitasking, by reading e-mail, listening to voicemail or completing other tasks all while the conversation is taking place.

Besides the fact that this is completely rude, it also does not allow the person to gain 100% of your attention which can lead to inaccurate communication, errors and loss of business. *Discipline yourself to focus and listen 100% to each person that takes the time to communicate with you.*

As we speak, thousands, maybe millions of talented employees are getting demoted, laid off or fired because of poor performance or diminished performance. Many times it can be accredited to the fact that in the beginning the employee set up a good habit of focusing 100% of their time to each task that they were being trained on and accountable for. But as business grew and as their responsibilities grew, their habit of focusing 100% did falter and as a result their performance suffered. If you haven't already, please start to implement this lesson. It will pay off tenfold and will also help to reduce the amount of projects you will have to "redo" later by getting the task done right the first time.

MANAGERS:

As a manager and mentor make sure you enforce this lesson of doing one task at a time by focusing 100% on each task. The results of your employee's performance reflects in your ability as a manager. Don't you want your employees to be running at peak performance with each and every task they complete? How would that impact your management performance record? Or your year end bonus? This lesson is worth passing on to your employees because it benefits everyone (you, your clients, your employees and the company).

The best way to make sure your employees will understand the value of this lesson is if you follow it yourself. Make a commitment to all of your employees by making them aware that you promise to give them 100% when they come in to speak to you. Show them what that looks like by turning your chair to pay direct attention to them. Don't keep typing or reading your e-mails. Ask that all of your calls be held until your discussions with them are over. Give each and every employee 100% attention so they know the importance of paying direct attention to a person. Be the influential role model by showing them how it is done. Your employees will learn to do the same to their co-workers and clients.

After reading this lesson, hopefully many people have just realized how rude they have been by reading e-mails or completing other tasks while listening to an employee, never mind the fact that they were not paying 100% to either task. The critical point to mention here is when managers don't focus 100% on an employee's needs, the result could be that the employees are going to treat their customers and co-workers the same way.

Trust me on this one; this is not a good habit to follow. Invest in your employees by showing them the value of focusing 100% of your attention to one task at a time. Start each meeting with each employee by looking at them not your computer and by listening to their needs 100% without interruption. The disciplined effort will pay off and your employees will have a good role model to follow.

Personal Note:

My daughter actually enforced this lesson with me a few years ago. One night after work, I was scrambling around in the kitchen trying to get dinner ready and Gracie, then 5 years old, started repeating, "Mommy . . . Mommy . . . Mommy . . . Mommy . . . Mommy!!! I kept answering her back by saying, "Yes, Gracie, what is it? I'm right next to you in the kitchen, I can hear you, what do you need?" Gracie then responded back by saying *"Mommy, look at me when I am talking to you."*

This was a good wake up call to me. It made me realize that if I was doing that to my precious five-year-old daughter then I surely was doing that on the job, too!

Thanks, Gracie!

Lesson 7

"The teacher will appear when the student is ready."
— unknown

HAVE YOU EVER ATTENDED a seminar with a co-worker and walked away with different information from the same speaker or read a book for the second time and understood facts and ideas that you did not understand the first time? Why does this happen? Simple. You were not tuned into the information because it did not apply to you or relate to anything currently on your mind. Usually you identify with something and are open to an idea when it applies to you personally. The "teacher" in the quote above is the vehicle delivering the message (book, story, speaker, lesson, etc.). The "student" is you because you are now open to learning the lesson, because it relates to something in your life now.

EMPLOYEES:

Every person that you meet can teach you something. Be open-minded, listen to people and be aware of different ideas and philosophies. I recently attended a meeting where the COO of Purdue Pharma spoke. He mentioned during his speech "no one is as smart as everyone." This statement is so simple yet so powerful. Have you ever noticed that the top performers in your company/industry are constantly reading books or attending seminars? By attending all the seminars and reading all the latest business books, they are constantly keeping up with the latest industry trends, equipping themselves with up-to-date tools and ideas, and keeping themselves motivated by interacting with others in the industry.

MANAGERS:

Once a month, try to introduce a new tool or principle to your staff to help them perform their jobs better. Some of these tools could be how to manage their time better, negotiate better, to increase self-motivation or to learn to close more sales. Any job can get stale quickly if there are no new ideas coming in. By constantly supplying new tools and principles to your employees, they in return will be more likely to stay interested in working for the company as well as being self-motivated and challenged by their positions. The employees will also learn to embrace changes as they occur with a positive outlook; from changes in software applications to changes in working hours to keep up with production. An employee who stays open minded to corporate policy changes certainly stands out in the crowd amongst the complainers who resent having to change old habits. It is a shame how many employees put themselves in jeopardy of losing their positions when they object to change. As a manager, encourage your employees to embrace changes early on in their career so they can see the value of new technology and new processes being implemented.

Reward your top employees by sending them to annual seminars or trade shows. The annual networking has a threefold effect to benefit your employees' morale, the company's process improvement levels and new technology awareness. In business change is good, healthy and inevitable. Accept it or lose fighting against it.

Lesson 8

Give examples as to why rules are in place.

Early on in my career I was always the person designated to train the new employees. The beginning of every training session always began with reviewing the rules of the company. As a trainer that wanted to make sure the new employees learned it right the first time, I always made a point of teaching the rules with an example behind each rule to help them understand the meaning behind why we have such rules in place. An example was always used so that the new employee could relate to the reasoning behind the rule(s) and the consequences that applied to them if they broke the rule(s).

For example: When a bartender is training on how to spot a patron that should be "shut off" (not served any more alcohol) because they drank too much, it is crucial for that bartender to understand the consequences of knowing that they could be sued if that patron leaves the bar and gets involved in a drunk driving accident or even worse if a person is injured or dies. As a trainer make sure that when you train new employees on policies and procedures that the new employee understands the consequences as to how it will relate to them if they don't follow the rules. It is very important in any industry to enforce a rule by making it real and tangible. The employee should be able to relate to the rule by understanding why it is in effect and how the rule came into effect. *This certainly helps to increase the chance of the employee's compliance with the rule when they fully understand the application of the rule, the history behind the rule and the consequences incurred if they violate the rule.*

EMPLOYEES:

From kindergarten, children are always taught to always ask questions and that there is no such thing as a stupid question. In the business world, if a rule just does not make sense or it conflicts with your values, discuss the rule. Find out why it is in place, especially if your trainer did not take the time to explain why it is in place. Most policies and procedures are not all written down. Some are just assumed and some are expected. Don't compromise your job because you don't understand a rule or policy. Ask questions. Naturally, there are going to be times when a policy or procedure is going to be bent to accommodate a client. Make those decisions wisely. Put yourself in the shoes of the owner of the company. Would they make the same decision? If the answer is no, then don't bend the rule. If the answer is yes, get permission and qualify why you are bending the rule.

MANAGERS:

When employees are being trained on the rules of the company, always tell them why the rules are in place. If possible, explain to them what specific event caused the implementation of the rule. If the actual event is top secret, then use a relative example, instead of just stating the rule. Using an example will help the employees to understand why the rule is in place and what the consequences are to them if they break the rule. The employee needs to realize "how that rule will affect them personally?" The answer is they will benefit from not getting into trouble like the first employee did that caused the rule to be implemented. If a manager or trainer just gives the rule, it does not give them reason not to do it. At the very least, sometimes they might have to make the mistake first before they believe in the rule. Prevent that from happening by giving them an explanation of the rules and you will save yourself hours of problem solving.

Lesson 9

When complimenting people, don't overdo it.

"Flattery is telling a person exactly what they already think of themselves."
— unknown

A WELL-KNOWN SALES TOOL that has been taught and practiced by millions of professionals for decades is that "if you want someone to like you or do business with you, then you should start off the conversation by saying their name and then by giving them an honest, sincere compliment."

To go one step further, it has also been suggested that when you enter a person's office or their house, look for something to compliment them on so that it will be a good icebreaker and allow the person to immediately like you. Unfortunately, this type of complimenting is often abused by sales people and is a quick turn off when it is overdone. I can recall a new salesperson that was working for me who within her first few days from hire would compliment my earrings or my clothes or my shoes at least once a day. I finally got to the point, after the third day where I could not even appreciate the compliment because it was so abused. My word of advice is to please be careful not to overdo the compliments because it can backfire. *When delivering compliments in any relationship, be honest, timely and tactful with the compliment and never overdo it.*

EMPLOYEES:

Complimenting a person is a great way to bond a relationship. Just be aware that overcomplimenting a person can be a total turnoff. No one wants to be labeled as "the slick salesman type" by overcomplimenting.

In addition, a compliment as harmless as "Sally, you look great in that suit", or "Sally, have you lost weight?" can be misinterpreted as a sexual harassment statement. It all depends on how it is said with the tonality of the voice and how the receiver interprets the comment. Please consult with your human resource manager for more information on sexual harassment training. Remember, no one likes to do business with a person they feel uncomfortable with. Watch what you say and how it is said to prevent any awkward situations.

MANAGERS:

Coach your employees to know when to deliver a compliment and to be aware that too many compliments can spoil a relationship. Be certain that all of your employees understand the consequences of overcomplementing a person, no matter if it is a client, colleague or manager. The consequences can change the dynamic of the relationship where the receiver will view the employee as disingenuous, all because they over did the compliments.

From a management perspective, one should also be careful how, when and why you compliment your employees. It is true that employees will value a good honest compliment over a small bonus. It is also a shame to hear many well-deserving employees state that they never once received a compliment from a superior. Please make sure you are not part of that statistic. Lead by example; deliver compliments when they are deserved. As a mentor, remember some of the compliments that you share with your employees will stay ingrained in your employees' memory causing them to continue to believe in themselves for a lifetime, and they will in return go above and beyond for you as a manager. This is not a bad consequence for just recognizing and acknowledging talent and hard work.

Lastly, in reference to complimenting, co-workers and employees must be careful how it is said because you never know if the person receiving the compliment might misinterpret the compliment. For example, if a woman returns back from maternity leave and a man says, "Sally, you look fantastic, you lost so much weight, you got your figure back." That type of compliment can be misinterpreted if Sally is offended by the compliment because of the tonality in the voice on how the statement was delivered. When in doubt about giving a compliment because a person might not take it the right way, *don't say the compliment.* Better safe than sorry. A misinterpreted compliment could cause them to feel embarrassed or humiliated and/or could spark a sexual harassment claim. No company likes to get that type of publicity. It is important that all employees and managers attend an annual sexual harassment seminar to ensure that every employee understands their rights to ensure that the office environment is not hostile.

Lesson 10

*In reference to attendance, make sure
you think of your co-workers before you call out sick!*

A TTENDANCE IS A MAJOR ISSUE with most companies. A surprising fact is that many of the people who make the wrong decisions about attendance by abusing the policy, honestly don't know they are doing anything wrong. Many times these employees or managers are just repeating what they saw their parents do. It is definitely the responsibility of the hiring manager to describe to each and every employee what is acceptable and what is not acceptable by using examples they can relate to. That way there is no misunderstanding between what the employee has seen in the past from their parental influence and what is expected from their current employer.

Fact: When an employee calls out sick, the job tasks that the employee was assigned to perform for that day will result in one of two scenarios. The first scenario that can occur is when the tasks that the employee was going to perform for that day go uncompleted. These uncompleted tasks can stall production, which could result in the customer being dissatisfied with delayed service and delivery from the company. This is not a good thing. The second scenario that can occur when an employee calls in sick and does not complete their required tasks for that day is when their work is distributed to another co-worker(s). This distribution of work creates an additional workload burden for the already busy staff member(s). The end result of having staff members overburdened can be a decrease in quality of the end product, an increase in work related injuries and a decrease in delivery of service, all of which negatively affects the company.

From an ideal perspective, what an employee should ask themselves when thinking about calling out sick is, "is it worth putting the extra burden on their co-workers? And would they want their co-workers to do the same to them?" Hopefully, the answer will be "no, I would not like to make other people suffer the consequences of my poor attendance attitude" and they will go to work.

The "sick days" that are being referred to here are not the days when an emergency happens or when a person is legitimately in bed with the flu; those are valid. The days that are being referred to specifically are the days when a person just does not feel like going to work because they feel tired or when they have a mild cold and they choose to use it as an excuse not to go to work. Hopefully, just the question alone of "do I want to force my co-workers to have to pick up my slack?" should be enough of a motivator to go to work and not call out sick.

The following are some generally observed correlations about attendance and employees:

- The happier the employee is on the job, the better the attendance.
- The unhappier the employee is on the job, the worse the attendance.
- People with poor attendance, missing more than 1 day a month consistently, do not stay in permanent or temporary jobs very long. In fact they usually never will keep a job longterm until they learn to make better decisions about attendance.

This cause and effect scenario should prompt all supervisors to review all of their employee's attendance records to identify any major red flags in attendance. It is always recommended even during the interview and on the first day of hire that every employee be instructed as to what is expected in regards to attendance. Specifically, the employee should be told that missing "x" amount of days in 3 months is unacceptable and will not be tolerated.

EMPLOYEES:

The following guideline has been put together to help employees understand general attendance expectations when beginning a new job.

- Make sure that the offer of employment is in writing and you have a copy of the attendance policy.
- Make sure all of the relevant information, in reference to holidays, vacations, sick days and personal days are mentioned and understood as to how they are earned and requested.
- Read the entire employee manual from front to back. If you don't understand a policy, then see Human Resources or your manager for clarification.
- It is imperative to know who to contact if you have an emergency when the office is closed. Have a list of names and numbers to contact from home when you need to call out.
- Don't ever "no show, no call." This means not showing up to work and not calling to say you will be absent. It is unacceptable and

could be grounds for termination (if proper documentation is not presented that excuses the employee of their absence). When an emergency happens, make every effort to inform management that you will not be in. Lack of communication can result in lack of employment.

- Memorize the company's toll-free 800 phone number. Don't know the number? Then call the toll free 800 directory at 1-800-555-1212 for the company's toll free listing.

- Always think of your co-workers when you are planning on calling out. Soul search with yourself to see if you really need to take the day off. Do the right thing by going to work if you physically can.

- If inclimate weather is forecasted, be prepared to still arrive to work on time by leaving 15 to 20 minutes earlier than ususal to allow for slower than usual travel time.

- Request to take time off in advance. Always put the request in writing and present to your manager weeks in advance.

- If you need to take time off for a doctor's appointment, try to schedule the appointment either first thing in the morning, during lunch or late in the day. Unless the appointment is out of town or you need to run other errands, there really is no reason to take an entire day off for a routine one hour appointment. Return to work after the appointment, if possible, to make up the time missed.

- Save your sick days for when you really need them. It is definitely encouraged by all human resources departments to take personal days. Personal days are great for the employee to take care of personal errands or to spend quality time with loved ones. The good thing about a personal day is that it is usually a planned day off so that the company has already prepared to expect you to be out.

- Always call your immediate manager when calling out, don't avoid your manager by calling a co-worker to tell them you will be out. The co-worker may forget to notify the manager and your job could still be in jeopardy for not calling the right person.

MANAGERS:

The most important task a manager should do to prevent poor attendance is to make sure that the employees know what the manager expects of them. Set the expectations by making sure the employees know that being absent more than a specific amount of days in three months is unacceptable. Make it clear that all employees are to call the manager or the next person in the chain of command when they do call out. Always provide a phone number to call when the office is closed as well as the toll free 800 number to the office. Let them know that a "no show no call" is grounds for termination.

Many companies these days are simply combining vacation, personal days and sick days into paid time off, so that employees start off the year knowing that they have a specific amount of days to take off. The incentive is to let the employees know that they *are* appreciated and *are* expected to take the time off and will always give management advance notice as to when they will be absent to reduce lost production time.

The time spent setting the attendance expectations to each member of your staff (hourly or salary) will reduce the confusion of what is acceptable and what is just downright abusive in reference to calling out or leaving early. Don't assume your employees already have the same good values about attendance. Many employees will repeat the same pattern of that of their parents, unfortunately some of those attendance values might not be so acceptable these days. So take the time to instruct your employees on what is acceptable with examples such as "calling out sick more than twice in a 3-month time frame is not acceptable" or "arriving late, taking a long lunch and leaving early to attend a dentist appointment all in the same day is totally unacceptable."

As a manager, make sure there are no misinterpretations as to what is expected from each employee's attendance during a fiscal year of employment. For some of your employees you will be reshaping their promotability and their career by changing old beliefs that are not acceptable in the workforce today. It is encouraged for all managers to have an active contact list of all employees with their home phone numbers in case an emergency arises.

Lesson 11

*"Treat every person you meet, as if they are
the most important person in the entire world
because to them they are."* — Earl Nightingale

N OT ONLY IS A NAME IMPORTANT to a person, but please remember that every person you meet thinks they are the most important person in the world and to them it is true. Take an honest interest in every person that you meet. There has to be something that person has experienced in their lifetime that you can learn from. Take advantage of it. It could be a unique approach on sales, musical interest, self-motivation, humor, exercise, health, adventure, self-empowerment, management skills, networking connection, etc. I have always believed that everything happens for a reason. Take advantage of every encounter.

At 21 years old, I worked in the healthcare industry for 1 year as an Ophthalmic Assistant. Some of the tests that I conducted on elderly patients lasted up to 45 minutes. There was often a lot of downtime in between each test result. I learned to take advantage of this downtime by asking the 70-, 80- and 90-year-old patients what life lessons they had learned that they could pass on to me. The responses were usually:

I wish I had:

- Spent more time with my family and friends.
- Stopped and smelled the roses more often.
- Not let people influence me from my dreams.
- Not worried about what other people thought of me.
- Taken better care of my health.

I cherished every conversation that I had with those patients and I bet that if you were to conduct the same questions with elderly people today, the answers would be the same or similar. Make a point of doing the things that you want to do now so that you don't end up with regrets later on in life. Listen to the advice of others — every person can teach you something of value if you let them.

EMPLOYEES:

When you are with your co-workers, ask them for any advice about the company or the job. Take advantage of their experiences; you don't have to necessarily accept their advice but at least take advantage of any information that they can give you to gain a different perspective. Let others talk about themselves; as previously mentioned everyone loves to talk about themselves and they like to share their experiences. By letting others talk, it will sometimes allow you to realize that other people are less fortunate than you, which will help to put your "problems" into perspective and also make you understand what your co-workers are experiencing in their lives. By allowing your co-workers to share an experience, it will also give your co-workers a feeling of being valued. With every conversation that I have with people, I always feel that there is something that you can take away from that meeting. Sometimes it is a fresh new approach on a subject and other times it will be a reinforcement of an idea already accepted by you that that person has reminded you of, positively or negatively.

In today's business market with technology evolving to such a high degree of intricacy, there are very few positions that a person can work in which they have no interaction with other co-workers. In most working environments, employees have to rely on each other to complete projects. This has increased the need for people to understand diversity issues between cultures in the work place. These basic skills are critical to help develop trust in one another when it comes to working together on a team. It is more common today to have a group of highly specialized employees working together in collaboration to complete a project because no one person can have all the answers for technology, finance, production, inventory, marketing, sales, etc. So take the time to get to know people. The time spent strengthening individual relationships will usually yield better results by increasing the understanding of each participant's responsibilities when on a project as well as increased communication and cooperation between departments.

"High potential employees" are employees that are identified within an organization for possessing the right educational background, work experience and skills that will allow them to move up in the ranks rapidly. If rapid promotion is on your career goal list and you match the organizations educational, work experience and skills requirements please be aware there is still more work in store for you to be recognized.

In general "high potential employees" must also be risk takers, possess strong values and be competent to lead. These selected employees are also evaluated by how well they get along with others and work together in a team environment. If you have a goal to be identified as a "high potential employee" take the time to evaluate if any of the areas mentioned might need some fine tuning. This is another example why employees need to be able to get along with others, not for the sake of having a better day at work but for the sake of being identified as a "high potential employee" because you do get along well with others. As I mentioned in the beginning of this book, *success in business all comes down to human relation skills.* You can be the smartest employee but if you don't know how to communicate or interact with people, it will get you nowhere. So invest in your co-workers, listen to their needs and find the value in their advice, everyone benefits from it in the long run.

MANAGERS:

Make sure that managers get together at least every month to exchange ideas and to strengthen the lines of communication in the company. During management meetings, make sure each and every manager communicates what is going on in their office or department. Usually, a manager will find out that a department or office has experienced a similar situation. The exchange of ideas and solutions are invaluable. Try to never miss a meeting. The exchange of ideas and experiences should always recharge the manager with a wealth of information and new ideas to bring back to their office. Make sure your company allows managers to interact face to face "on open discussions" at least on a monthly basis. The meeting will always pay for itself and more.

The exchange of ideas and experiences should also be shared with your employees in the office. There is a wealth of information in a roomful of employees, especially employees that can share ideas they learned from previous employers and companies. Always encourage your employees to bring to the table suggestions on how to improve the office or increase business. It will bring added value to the office and make the employee feel important and contribute his/her ideas to the office. By allowing employees to contribute to the growth of the office, it also gives them a sense of satisfaction in their job, which helps to reduce turnover and increase employee satisfaction and morale.

Lesson 12

Don't stress out while "in the weeds."

I LEARNED A TWOFOLD LESSON about stress from "being in the weeds" while working in a restaurant during my college days. "Being in the weeds" literally is when you start to feel overwhelmed because you have too many tasks to complete at once and you don't know which task to do first. The only way people of all industries learn to cope under this intense pressure is to develop the habit of prioritizing each and every task in order of importance and by not letting the stress get to you. Have you ever witnessed a waitress or waiter crying in a busy restaurant? Then you probably witnessed a breakdown from "being in the weeds."

I recall an experience early on in my career as a waitress when an elderly female patron was unacceptably and inexcusably rude while giving me a dinner order during a hectic dinner rush. Shortly before I approached the table, I was informed that the kitchen was at least an hour behind, so any fast service I was going to give this patron was never going to be good enough. By the time the food arrived, she was even more rude and impatient than I ever could have imagined. As I quickly approached the table, I started to prepare myself mentally for the abuse that I was about to encounter from this mean, rotten and nasty woman. Then it dawned on me. This was only a meal, one of thousands of meals that this patron will have in her lifetime. I realized I had two choices, I could decide to let her rude manners affect me or I could decide to stay neutral and accept that she would be fed and gone within the next hour. I decided not to allow her rude manners affect me personally after I realized she would probably not even remember the service, good or bad. I took the high road and decided to *still* treat her with respect. Surprisingly, by the end of the meal she lightened up, complemented the chef and became a regular customer to the restaurant for years after that event.

Fortunately, this twofold lesson of learning how to deal with "being in the weeds" and with rude people was priceless to me. I can't emphasize enough that if a stressful situation has you "in the weeds" mentally, *remember* if it is not life threatening, please don't let it affect your state of mind. View the situation from a lifetime viewpoint and realize that this specific incident is just a blip of their lifetime and yours.

Undoubtedly, if there is something that you can learn from a negative situation, do so, it will make you that much stronger the next time you encounter a situation that is similar. Ironically, by building up your level of experience, you might even get to the point where you thrive under high pressure, high stress environments.

EMPLOYEES:

Please exercise the following advice the next time you find yourself "in the weeds." When things start to get out of control to the point where you feel overwhelmed try the following: take a deep breath and put everything in perspective. Ask yourself, "in the grand scheme of life, how important is this one situation?" If the answer is "not that important at all" then complete the task by realizing that you don't have to break down to the mental pressure because the tasks seem too big to tackle at that point. Instead focus on your tasks, write them down if you have to, prioritize and complete them, one at a time in order of importance. Next, get through the day. At the end of the day, evaluate what you did to get out of "the weeds." Was it the most effective way to manage your time? What could you have done better? What could you have prepared for in advance? Congratulations, you just grew from that experience. The next time you are "in the weeds" you will be better prepared, more in control and able to surprisingly take on more tasks if needed.

In an office environment, a great way to prevent mental meltdowns from "being in the weeds" with projects and reports is to request assistance from another employee who might not be so busy. If that is not an option, just realize that you can only do one thing at a time. Decide which tasks take priority by identifying which tasks have immediate deadlines, are critical to satisfying an important customer's needs, will produce a substantial cost savings or profit, or will save your job. Any project that is a long shot or not urgent should take a backseat until the priority tasks are done first. By following this twofold lesson of learning how to effectively work "in the weeds" and to not let your mental state get affected by the stress, your career will be more enjoyable and your competence level will continue to increase.

MANAGERS:

Train your employees on the importance of not stressing out over the little things. Make them realize that by stressing out over being overworked or having too many things to do at once just wastes time and energy. Teach your staff to prioritize and to know when to delegate their responsibilities to someone else in order to get the job done. Always cross train your employees to make sure that other employees can cover for each other when needed. Please enforce with your employees the importance of giving 100% on each task that they do. Don't let them only give 50% or 60% effort on each task just because they are "in the weeds."

Your employees should know that if they can't give each task 100% of their effort then maybe they should ask for an extension or ask someone else to take on the project.

Naturally, it is part of human nature to make mistakes, so expect mistakes to happen. Through experience we all grow. Some of the best training has been educated and enforced by on-the-job mistakes. As a manager, capture the moment when a mistake is made by making sure the employee or employees learn from the mistake immediately. Make sure they understand the consequences if the same mistake is repeated. This discussion will help prepare everyone in the future when they are faced with a similar situation.

A great idea is to ask all your employees at the end of each week to write down what lesson(s) they learned that week. Record those lessons in a journal; it is priceless information to keep. Later, transfer all of those lessons into a training manual for the employees to review. Talk about those experiences in employee meetings to make everyone aware of situations that might happen on the job.

By discussing the mistakes of others in group settings, it should make all of the employees realize that they are not infallible. Hopefully, all of your employees should feel confident enough to know that their job is not in jeopardy if they make a mistake. As a trainer and a manager, I can vouch that it is impossible to prepare each employee for every unique situation they will encounter on the job. The more experiences and mistakes that you can share with your employees, the better off your employees will be when they are faced with scenarios that they have not been trained to deal with yet.

*"Experience is a hard teacher, because she gives
the test first and the lesson second."*
— Vernon Saunder Law

*"God, thank you for the mistakes, because without mistakes,
I would not have learned a thing!"*
— Bob Beverage

Lesson 13

*When the time is right, place the blame
on company policy to reduce
misdirected criticism and undue stress.*

MANY TIMES THROUGHOUT a person's career on a daily or weekly basis, they will have to deliver information to a client, customer, employee or even a co-worker that will make both parties feel uncomfortable, awkward and stressed. Some work related examples of situations that make both parties feel uncomfortable are the following:

- When an increase in production needs requires employees to be forced by managers to work mandatory overtime. Managers feel uncomfortable to force their employees to work overtime and the employees feel anger and resentment towards unexpected overtime.
- When an employee is terminated because he/she broke a company policy. The person involved in the firing is uncomfortable and certainly the employee is uncomfortable.

The easiest way to proceed with the awkward situation is to focus on the *violation of company policy. Do not at this time interject any personal emotion about the situation.* Just deliver the information that should be stated, let the client, customer, manager or employee digest the information and follow up with proper paperwork or actions. Again, refer to company policy. Do not interject your personal feelings to make the person feel better.

The following is a step by step process on how to apply the blame to company policy instead of internalizing undue stress from a disgruntled customer or employee.

Step #1:

Take the emotion out of personally getting blamed for the policy by letting the client, customer or employee know that you "understand how they feel and that you agree that the new policy of _____ is strict." However, let them know that you are just doing your job by following the rules enforced by company policy in order to keep your job.

Step #2:

If the client or employee is still upset, suggest to them that they write a letter to the company. Provide them with the necessary contact information and be sure to follow-up on their complaint personally.

Step #3:

By following these steps of putting the blame on company policy and letting them know that you sympathize with them, undue stress can be prevented. Unfortunately, many employees that participate on a daily basis with clients (such as call centers) internalize the constant negativity which is thrown at them. This constant negativity will burn out the employee on the job quickly if they don't use this approach; or at least a similar one to reduce the stress load.

This lesson should not be confused with accepting blame when blame is due or when the situation can be resolved by assuming the blame. It is a different situation, however, when a policy must be enforced such as when an employee skips work for two days in a row without calling the company. Any person of authority conducting the termination can and should blame company policy by stating that "you have violated a company policy on absenteeism and you are therefore terminated." (Managers, please make sure your company has an employee handbook that defines and details company policies.)

For all of you who are in sales, this lesson can be a valuable learning curve for you. Always be prepared that your clients will try to negotiate a lower price on your proposed product. If you are confident that you do not want to lower your price, tell the client that "unfortunately, the company policy does not allow me to go any lower than I have already gone." It will take the ownership off your shoulders and make the client realize you have done all you could to give the best price. Most of the time, you will still sell the product at your price if you successfully convinced your client that your customer service is better than your competitor's.

When you stand firm and don't lower your price, you also show respect for yourself, the people that make the product and for your customer service team. Do not reduce your price if your product is as good as you believe it is. That will convince your client that your product is worth every dollar that they spend on it.

MANAGERS:

There will be times when you will have to request your employees to work overtime. One of the best ways to successfully handle the situation so that everyone agrees to work the mandatory overtime is to state that it is company policy. If it is not company policy, then somebody better take the blame. Have the president or the CEO make a statement that it is mandatory that everyone work overtime this weekend, including management. By putting the blame on the CEO or "company policy" it allows the staff to not personally hold a grudge against the person delivering the message (usually the manager). As a manager, it is critically important that the staff understands why the overtime is mandatory. For example "the CEO of the company is requiring that all employees work overtime this week to make up for lost production due to the two day power failure, which affected our production runs this week. If the time is not made up, then our clients will not receive their products in time for the holiday season and that will affect our year end profits, which could affect our year end bonuses. Are there any questions?" By stating the message this way it allows the employees to understand where the order is coming from and why. Therefore, the pressure should be taken off the person delivering the message so that business can continue as usual without any undue stress.

You may ask yourself "what if the CEO does not want the blame or did not place the order?" This suggestion of stating that the CEO of the company is enforcing the policy should only be used when you have no doubt that it is true. If there is a decision that you make as a manager that is being enforced by you, then make it known that it is coming from you. Please be advised that this lesson is to be used when a policy needs to be accepted immediately by everyone and there is no other alternative but to enforce the policy. As a reminder to help to alleviate undue stress on the job, coach your employees to expect customers to be confrontational. Train your employees not to internalize negative confrontations but instead to *refer to company policy to place the blame* and to educate the customer. Remind them to state, "I am only following company policy."

In addition, it is wise to have your employees capture all of the negative complaints in a log book. This log book should be reviewed on a daily or weekly basis because this information can lead to valuable insight as to what the customer is actually looking for in improved service. If some of the complaints about company policy are valid, these recorded complaints could give the company more market share by servicing the customer better.

Life Lesson #2

*Get yourself into a positive frame
of mind while under stress.*

ACT: AN EMPLOYEE'S MOOD is going to be constantly attacked or acted upon by hundreds of different stressors throughout the day. These stressors could be from an upset client, a boss that is dissatisfied with production, computer failure problems, copier machine or fax machine crashes, overtime requirements, internal communication breakdowns, personality conflicts on the job, personal problems at home and or health problems. The important lesson here is that the employee must learn not to let these stressors affect their mental state or attitude for the entire day. Remember a stressor can only affect a person's state of mind if they allow it to.

If the situation is at work, let's say from a difficult client, the employee needs to learn to deal with the problem and move ahead without getting emotionally charged from the interaction. Difficult situations, stressors and obstacles are all part of life. The only way to effectively deal with them is keep a positive state of mind. Employees need to learn to deal with them effectively because these situations are never going to stop coming, as a matter of fact the more experience you gain in the industry the more problems you learn to solve. This is true in any industry and that is why a person with a lot of experience in an industry is so valuable, because they can quickly deliver a solution to a common situation and move on to the next task. Most often times, they go one step further and prevent the problem from occurring because they know how to prevent the situations from becoming troublesome before it occurs (preventive maintenance).

Every employee should now realize that the key to staying happy on the job when situations arise is to approach every situation as a learning process. These learning processes are a way to constantly push out their comfort zone, exercise one's training and increase one's capabilities of dealing with difficult people and situations.

During a difficult situation, employees should make sure they understand both sides of the situation, make an informed decision, learn from it and are ready for the next situation without having to affect their mood or pass off any negative comments to co-workers or spouses. Many problems start to fester and affect employee morale when nothing is done, such as a report that stays untouched on a desk for weeks while causing the employee to stress out each day and get in a bad mood. Instead of stressing over having it on the desk, they should schedule the time out of their day to finish the report and stay happy. Life does not have to be that difficult. Remember the report did not make the employee stress out, the employee made himself stress out because of what he allowed himself to feel. If he doesn't allow the stressor to act upon his mental state, then his mental state stays unaffected. It is important to note that many employees limit their potential of advancement because they can't handle the stress when the pressure is on. This should be reason enough for all employees to learn the importance of dealing with stress effectively. They need to learn to deal with stress by not allowing it to affect their state of mind by keeping the emotion out of it.

Now that employees understand the value of not allowing stressors to affect their mental state, there is one more topic to talk about: nervousness. Nervousness is an exciting state to be in because it can also mean that the person is about to experience something that they can grow from or learn from, if they handle it correctly. Let's use an example of a candidate preparing for an interview with a new company.

An interviewee, John Smith is extremely nervous while sitting in a company lobby preparing for his interview. His hands are wet and clammy. His mouth is parched, yet he is too nervous to ask for a cup of water. His mind is spinning because he is trying to remember all the canned answers he had prepared; to answer such questions as "why are manholes round?" and "if he were an animal what kind of animal would he be?"

At the same time he is also trying to recite the company's mission statement, the CEO's name and the products the company manufactures. Needless to say, John is a mess.

Ironically, John knows he can handle the job responsibilities, if only he could master the art of interviewing. So what can he do to overcome and reduce the stress of the interview? Simple, while John is in the lobby preparing for the interview, he should recall a major event in his life when he felt a sense of accomplishment. This major event could have been when he earned an award, completed a project, graduated from college, received a promotion, bought a house, etc. Interestingly, the major event does not have to be work related. What is important is for John to bring himself back into that moment to remember that feeling of accomplishment when he felt on top of the world, confident, and able to accomplish anything he set his mind to. That feeling of accomplishment should temporarily force John to feel more confident, less nervous and more certain of his skills during his interview. This technique can be used throughout the interview as well. Whenever John starts to feel unsure of himself during the interview, all he needs to do is to quickly recall a major accomplishment to reinforce in himself that he is capable, confident and the right man for the job because of his memory of accomplishing other goals that he set his mind to.

This exercise can be used by anyone at anytime throughout the day, before or during a meeting, competition, exam, power lunch, etc. If you are in sales, try this before you make your next sales call by bringing yourself to a confident state of mind before the next call. You should notice that you will be sitting up straighter, speaking with more confidence, handling objections better or even standing up to make that call because you just feel so confident in yourself! Try it today, get yourself into a positive frame of mind all day by remembering a past event that you accomplished. The key is not to let anyone or anything take that feeling away. Your co-workers will wonder what has gotten into you; ironically, it was always in your mind only it was stored away until now!

"A truly happy person is one who can enjoy the scenery on a detour."
— unknown

Lesson 14

Stear clear of gossip and uncomfortable confrontations will steer clear of you.

THIS LESSON OF NOT GOSSIPING plays a dual role on the job and socially. I personally learned this lesson the hard way when I was twelve years old attending middle school in Mannheim, Germany. There I was outside in the schoolyard standing in a circle with some of the most popular girls in school.

A character flaw that I tended to overlook in my "friends" was that they tended to gossip about other people just to keep a conversation going. During one conversation, in order to seem as if I was "part of the team," I started to the rantipole antics in order to participate in the conversation about a specific girl "Susan" in school who I personally did not know.

The following day, Susan, who heard through the grapevine that I talked about her in an "unappreciative manner," sent a widespread message throughout the school that her and her friends were going to beat me up near the school buses after school. To say the least, I was terrified. Once the dismissal school bell rang, I ran from my last class to the school bus as fast as I possibly could to avoid any conflict. Unfortunately, once the girls realized that I was on the bus, they went after my oldest sister, Lorraine, who was right in front of the bus. Lorraine was beat up right in front of me. I tried to get off the bus to help my sister but the driver would not let me get off. That was one of the worst days of my life, yet a great lesson was learned! (sorry Lorraine)

I learned the lesson that day to never gossip about people. Please follow the old adage, "if you don't have anything good to say, don't say anything at all." This applies across the board to employees, managers and owners. Another good piece of advice that I picked up along the way from an unknown source (Dale Carnegie?) is "if the person that is being talked about is not there to defend themselves, then don't talk about them."

EMPLOYEES:

This rule is straightforward: *don't gossip on the job.* Relieve yourself of undue stress in the office by not engaging in office gossip. If you are engaged in a conversation where gossip is introduced, don't agree to it, add to it or repeat the gossip. Instead just stay quiet or walk away. Your co-workers will have more respect for you if you stay neutral and don't participate in office gossip.

In addition, if you personally hear that someone has verbally criticized you, please remember this principle that Dale Carnegie preached for years, that "unjust criticism is often a disguised compliment." In other words, if someone criticizes another person, it is usually because that person is jealous of something that the other person has. Ironically, if you hear that someone has verbally criticized you and you know that the criticism is false, consider yourself flattered that someone is so caught up in your actions that they have to engage in criticism against you. I once had an employee who took care of my accounts while I went away on vacation for a week. That week turned out to be a very busy week, on top of a heavy account load to start with and the employee did a fabulous job at it. When I returned from vacation, I was informed that she was being called a "mini Lisa" and "overachiever" because she was busy working all week and did not socialize with the other members of the office. When I heard that the employee was called that, I told her, "Wow, what a great compliment to you! Don't be insulted by the comment but instead be flattered. They are jealous that you were able to handle all of my tasks and yours at the same time." Soon after, that same employee was officially promoted to acting office supervisor whenever I was not in the office.

MANAGERS:

Lead by example; don't get involved in office gossip. Remember, anything that you do or say will be followed. If you gossip, then your employees will think it is okay to gossip. If you don't gossip, then your employees will know that their leader does not promote gossip. It will cause your employees to respect you more for your integrity and give them an example to follow. This highly valued leadership quality of not gossiping will also increase trust in the office, which will only increase employee morale and communication.

"More people are run down by gossip than by automobiles."
— Leopold Fechtner

"It is much easier to be critical than it is to be correct."
— Benjamin Disraeli

"A gossip is a person who can give you all the details
without knowing any of the facts."
— Leopold Fechtner

Lesson 15

Squeal if it protects you and others.

I T IS INEVITABLE THAT there are going to be times when an employee or manager will observe an employee conducting an illegal action that is against company policy. For example, one might witness an employee stealing or "borrowing" items from the company stockroom without checking them out properly. So what is the witness to do? Is it the witness's responsibility to report the incident? Should the witness look the other way and not report the incident so that they are not labeled as a "tattletale", "whistle-blower" or "snitch"?

What the witness has to realize is this: if everyone in the company did the same illegal "take away" from the company, there would certainly be less office supplies to work with which would affect everyone. In addition, "if that employee has just been caught by you stealing company property, then what else have they stolen without being caught?" Is this the type of person you want working with you? I don't think so. As the law predicts, when a person is caught stealing or breaking into a house, it is usually not the first time that they did it. If they got away with it in the past, the chances that they will do it again are pretty high.

Another question the witness needs to ponder is "if I owned the company and I witnessed my own employee stealing from me, what would I do?" The answer is usually pretty clear now as to which action to take.

If an employee witnesses an illegal act, they should be aware from management that it certainly is okay to report the incident anonymously.

Another type of potential loss that occurs on the job is when one employee shares with a co-worker that they are interviewing with the competition. This certainly puts the employee that is told this information in an awkward situation, in the sense that the co-worker might take a client list with them to the competition, which could hurt the current company financially.

So what is the employee to do? The best answer I can give is to *think like an owner again.* If you were the owner and you found out that an employee of yours was interviewing with the competition, what would you do? Well, if the employee wasn't productive, then it isn't a concern but a blessing. However, if the employee is productive, then it is a major concern. (Many companies will have "non-compete legal contracts" that help to protect their client base from being stolen in cases like this.)

Getting back to the question at hand, if the employee who has admitted that they are interviewing with the competition is considered a threat if they leave the current company, then it is suggested that management should find out.

On a personal level, I have had several employees over the years that have come to me to confide about an employee of ours who was interviewing with the competition. Whenever we felt it was a direct threat and we had proof that the interviews had taken place, we let them go. My best advice for employees who are interviewing with the competition is to not let anyone know. When it comes to jobs and money, people will turn on you to protect their own investment in the company. You can't blame them, they are just protecting themselves.

EMPLOYEES:

Don't steal from your current employer. Think like an owner; you would not want to catch your employees stealing from you, so don't steal from your employer. When employees steal, it affects the bottom line; it can make the difference as to whether the company has a bountiful supply closet that an employee can access at any time or a locked supply closet that can only be accessed through a purchase order request approved from management.

Fact: Trust is the hardest bond to build back up with a person; don't ever let someone get the impression that they can't trust you by stealing from them. The price is too costly and whatever is stolen is never worth the consequences, especially if the person is legally convicted of the crime. Criminal backgrounds can and do tarnish careers. Stay trustworthy!

MANAGERS:

Keep an open door policy with your employees. Let them know that you appreciate it when they confide in you about illegal actions that have taken place in the office. Be sure to let your employees know that you trust them and that they can trust you. The suggested weekly meetings with your employees on a one on one basis will help you as a manager to stay on top of any activity from disloyal employees. As a manager, constant communication is also essential with your employees to prevent internal conflicts, tension or misunderstandings.

In other words, communicate with your employees to help eliminate the small problems so that they don't turn into bigger problems that could result in employee turnover and lost business. Also, consider creating a code of business principles that would include a discussion on "squealing" and what is expected of employees, anonymously or not. Enforce that everyone (employees, managers, owners and/or the executive board) must comply with the all the principles before they start working for the company. In addition, require that everyone sign off on the document(s) to confirm that they have read, understood and agree to comply with the principles while employed by the company. This action will help to encourage those who would be reluctant to speak up because they did not want to be labeled as a squealer or whistle-blower. By creating a code of business principles that discusses the expectations of squealing, it will now be a requirement to squeal based on the principles that they agreed to follow when they were hired on, no exceptions.

Lesson 16

Foul mouths are such a turnoff.

I N MOST PROFESSIONAL business environments, it is not appropriate to swear or curse. It is a well-known fact that employees with a broad vocabulary are always perceived as being more intellectual than those who have a limited vocabulary. This should be enough of a reason not to swear but unfortunately for many people it is not. I recall hearing about a recent study that proved there is a direct correlation between vocabulary size and promotablity. Interestingly, when two candidates of equal skill were compared to each other, the candidate with the larger vocabulary had the better chance of receiving the promotion. Do you ever wonder why most CEO's have a broad vocabulary? What do you think came first? The job or the broad vocabulary?

The English language has almost a million words. Get creative and describe your feelings; there is nothing more of a turnoff than someone who uses foul language on a repetitive basis. Often times the person using the vulgarities is not even aware of how often they swear. One of the biggest turnoffs and insults to a person that does not swear is to have a person use profanity at them. On a professional basis, don't take the chance of not bonding with a client by offending them with vulgarities. *Just think,* some clients might make a decision not to go with a specific account representative because they were insulted by their foul mouth. That should be reason enough to think of a better word instead of a swear word to describe your feelings.

It has also been observed throughout the ages that people who are not in control of their feelings are more inclined to use swear words, and people who are in control of their feelings are less likely to use swear words. Can you think of a person who meets one of these profiles?

EMPLOYEES:

If a person swears in front of you, kindly let them know that you would prefer that they refrain from swearing. If a client of yours is swearing, however, don't say a word. You never want your client to think that you are above them by putting them down for their use of language. Take the time to increase your vocabulary by learning a new word each day. You might just find a word that better describes your feelings than what the old "four letter" words did.

MANAGERS:

When delivering speeches and carrying on everyday interoffice communications with employees or fellow managers, don't swear or use curse words in your memos. You will gain more respect from your staff if you use a broad vocabulary to describe your feelings. Again, it is no coincidence that people with a broad vocabulary get promoted quicker than people of the same education but with a limited vocabulary.

A creative way to enforce a "no swearing rule" is by having a swear jar in the office. For every swear word said by an employee or manager, they have to donate 1 dollar into the jar. At the end of the year, the money is given to a local charity. This helps to enforce with all of the staff that swearing is not an acceptable business practice and it also helps to teach the employees to stay in control of their feelings.

FYI: You can also use this same jar for attendance. Whenever an employee comes in late, make them pay $5 to the charity jar. It will help to enforce the importance of not being late to work and meetings.

Life Lesson #3

*Don't quit your favorite job because
you need to make more money to get out of debt!*

I WISH I WOULD HAVE KNOWN this lesson years ago. For the past 8 years, my husband and I had been financially living the life that we believed was the right way to live. We finally got into a community that we liked and in a house that we felt we could call home, after a little remodeling of course.

As our first year went past in the house, a strange thing started to happen to our finances. As our income gradually increased over the years, so did our bills. It seemed as if every week we were never getting ahead and every week we were working to pay off our credit cards. Our mortgage, car payments and day-care expenses were bills that we had accepted to have to pay but our credit card payments were not acceptable; on the contrary they became unacceptable. Over the course of 8 years from home improvements, shopping sprees, vacations, trips and dining out we had accumulated over 5 credit cards with balances all or close to their limit.

This shocking credit card debt was now controlling our lives. In addition, it irrationally caused us to think we had to make more money to pay off our debt, even though our income was well above average. This thought process was causing us to think that one of us had to leave our current job that we loved, to find another job that would pay more money just to pay off our credit card debt. The crazy realism was that we *didn't need to make more money, quit our current jobs or take on another job part time. Realistically, all we needed to do was get rid of our debt!* Does this sound familiar?

So for the next few months, we agreed to make the largest monthly payment on all of our credit cards. We also agreed to put ourselves on a budget, stop dining out and reduced our spending drastically. To our surprise over the next few months the credit card balances were barely going down. This was due to the high interest rates on the cards. How defeating this situation was. We were sacrificing, not spending, making the payments and after all that, the payments were barely making a dent.

My husband, George, suggested we look into a debt consolidation loan but I just couldn't do it. Why would I allow someone to pay off my debt so that I can pay them more money for the same debt? No, I had seen too many people fall into that trap of thinking they were getting themselves out of debt with a debt consolidation loan when all they are doing was paying more money for the same debt but just extending it over a longer period of time to pay it back. Even though debt consolidation loans work for thousands of people in certain financial situations, for me and my family it was not an option. I had made a decision that I would rather struggle for the next 2 years to pay off all of my credit cards than to have to work for the next 15 years giving my weekly paycheck to a bank for a debt consolidation loan, paying back more in interest than what I had originally borrowed.

A few months later, in the summer of 2004, we were fortunate enough to be introduced to a program called "Transforming Debt into Wealth" by John Cummuta. After listening to this program on CD, it helped to reinforce my stand on refusing to give in to a debt consolidation loan to pay off my credit card debt. This program specifically educates people on how to pay off multiple credit card debt by focusing on one card at a time. It works by paying a maximum payment each month on one card and only paying the minimum payments on the rest of the cards until the cards are paid off one by one. The principles in the program are easy to follow and relatable. Excitedly, we decided to apply the principles of the program by identifying which card we wanted to get rid of first. Surprisingly, by following the program for only 4 months, adhering to a strict budget and making only the minimum payments on 4 of the 5 cards, we successfully paid off and closed our highest interest rate credit card. In December of 2004 we paid off our second highest interest rate card and as of April, 2005 we have successfully eliminated half of our credit card debt! The important lesson here is that we paid off this debt without earning any more money, we just found a better way to pay off the debt without having to take a loan. George and I have projected that we will be debt free from our credit cards by December 2005. The program works, try it today.

In addition, this program has also shown us how to pay off our 15-year mortgage in 7 years. Once again, I highly support this program; to learn more about John Cummuta and his debt management program go to www.nightingale.com/tdiw.

So what does this have to do with being motivated? Quite a bit if you are struggling to make ends meet. This is because 97% of Americans have chased the American dream of buying a house, having at least two car payments, carrying a revolving debt on several credit cards and paying off school loans. If you are fighting with your spouse or just stressing out every week about how you are going to make more money to get yourself out of debt then this life lesson is for you.

The first step is to realize that millions of people are in your situation and that there is a solution. It will take discipline but there is a way out without having to change jobs or take on a second job. My husband and I have only one regret about our financial debt experience; we wish we would have had better discipline when it came to using credit cards. We both agree that because we knew we were making a moderate income between the both of us, we figured we could always afford to buy what we needed on credit. Boy, were we wrong! We have calculated that for everything we have bought on our credit cards over the past few years, we have already paid double because of the interest and the length of time we carried the cards without paying them off.

George and I are now extremely grateful because we finally realized that we don't need to make more money to be happier. By disciplining ourselves to stay committed to our new debt management plan, ironically, our relationship between each other has improved. Instead of reluctantly writing out the credit card bills each month we actually look forward to making the monthly payments. Our perception of paying our bills has transformed because the balances are actually going down at a noticeable rate and now finally there is an end in sight to the debt completely.

If there is anything that you take away from this life lesson it is this: *don't change your job because of your debt.* If you love your job, your family, where you live and the amount of quality time you spend with family, don't give that up. Instead give up paying too much for what you buy. Pay cash for everything, use the credit cards only for emergencies and discipline yourself with your spending habits. As John Cummuta says, "don't compete with the Joneses". By reducing the amount of debt you owe, you will certainly live a less stressful life. It is surprising to realize that you don't need to have a lot of money to live richly you just need to stay out of debt. In this case, less is more!

Lesson 17

"Learn to respond, not to react."

— unknown

THE FOLLOWING LESSON of learning to "respond to pressure situations instead of reacting" is a classic business lesson that has been handed down by the true professionals of the business world for generations. When this lesson is followed on a daily basis, the results will be that an employee or manager will be less stressed, more in control and competent in their current position. Co-workers also gain an extra bonus when employees and managers adopt this new way of responding to situations because they become more of a pleasure to work with. Instead of constantly being in reaction mode, they are in "responsive" mode, which keeps every one calm and on a professional level.

Have you ever worked with a person who constantly reacted to situations by flailing their arms, violently shouting profanities or by slamming down the phone and so on? Did that help to solve the problem? Probably not, yet so many people seem to think it is their right to act that way on the job. Is it? No!

So why do so many people "lose it" when problems arise? One theory is that they don't know any other way because that is what their parents or previous bosses did, so they think it is okay or the right thing to do. An important point of this lesson is to realize and accept that problems are always going to continue coming your way. Some problems will be big, some small, some health-related and others financial-related. It is all part of life to deal with problems and to learn from them.

So if by chance you are experiencing a new problem for the first time, try this new approach of *accepting the problem.* Instead of getting upset about the problem, learn to deal with the problem by responding to the problem and begin to figure out how to deal with the problem. This new approach might just save your health, sanity, reputation and job.

The following is an example of how to respond on the job to a situation instead of reacting.

The next time a client calls in upset because something is not going right, respond to the client by being courteous, concerned and understanding. Do not become defensive to the client because *that* will not solve the problem. Remember, the customer is always right.

FACT: Often people make the mistake of not allowing themselves to be wrong. This is why so many companies lack good customer service. It is because the receiver allows their ego to get in the way of a business transaction that, in reality, means absolutely nothing in the meaning of life. Unfortunately, it does cause the company to suffer by often losing a customer because they were not treated correctly. This is not the time for the receiver of the call to play the "I am right you are wrong" role.

The following statement should be posters in every company:

"The customer is always right or the customer will leave! Forget about who is right or wrong and treat the customer well."

This statement would be a constant reminder to employees and managers not to react to clients but to professionally respond. This understanding alone separates the professionals from the standard average employee. As a motivated employee or manager who wants to move up in the ranks, please make sure that you understand the following statement. In order to learn to respond to a situation, a person needs to not scream at a client or assume the client is wrong. Instead, they need to listen to them, not interrupt them and hear them out. Once the client has stated their frustration, the employee needs to let the client know that you personally feel _____ (pick a word: horrible, upset or frustrated) that the following situation has occurred and that you will follow up with corrective action immediately. Again, this is not the time to tell the client that they are wrong or that you want to show the client how much smarter you are than them. Instead, it is the time to show the client how professional you are and how well trained you are in dealing with situations.

Listed below are the following proven steps that should be implemented to train an employee or manager to respond correctly in a negative situation.

1) Allow the client to state their feelings.
2) Immediately agree with them that you understand how they feel and would react the same way under the same conditions.
3) Try to set up an appointment to meet with the client, in person if possible, to gain all the facts of the situation and to let them know

how serious you take their account. Otherwise, take down all the information at that time.

4) Make sure you have all the correct contact information, with correct name spelling, title, phone number, e-mail address and mailing address; gather all the information and facts from both sides. Try to meet with them one on one.

5) Give the client a certain time frame to expect a follow-up response (a few hours, a few days, etc.).

6) Research the facts, follow up on the matter and find a solution.

7) Contact the client with the correct response and remind them that you would have reacted the same way based on the circumstances.

8) Send a thank-you card to the client for bringing the situation to your attention.

9) Change any processes in the company that might need improvement to prevent this error from occurring again. Request the need for new company training, if possible.

10) *Realize that everyday does not have to be a day in which you show a person that you are smarter than them or better off than them. Instead, let other people have their "time in the limelight" over issues that in the grand scheme of life have no bearing on anything personal. (I wish more people followed this advice.)*

EMPLOYEES:

This lesson is critical to follow and it needs to be practiced not only with your clients but also in the office with co-workers and superiors. Due to communication errors, equipment failures or attendance problems there will be multiple times that something will not go your way. It is especially in times likes these that you need to learn to respond instead of reacting to situations.

The following is another example that frequently happens on the job: A new office procedure is implemented and your first response is to feel angry or confused about the new "improvement" because it causes you to change your work pattern, which in the short run does not benefit you. Remember do not react by putting on a sour face or rolling your eyes in frustration. Instead, accept the change and be open-minded. Processes don't get changed to cause more problems. They get changed to improve efficiency. So, if the new process or change is not immediately beneficial, stay positive and try sitting down with the person who has implemented the change to gain their reason and viewpoint about the new process. By discussing the concerns and implementation process of the new procedure, new light will usually be shed on the internal operations of the business that might not have been revealed before to the employee. Once the entire picture is viewed, it makes it easier for the employee to understand the reason for the necessary change and to willingly accept the changes. All of this can happen when a person responds to a new situation instead of reacting to it. It is, once again, highly encouraged to speak to the person who is in charge of the change, in person. (Do not publicly critize them in front of co-workers.)

Another example: The next time you have an irate customer on the phone that is yelling vulgarities and threatening to call the Better Business Bureau, remember this time honored lesson and learn to respond to the customer by staying calm and concerned. Don't by any means treat the customer the way they are treating you, this will only add fuel to the fire. Remember, fires eventually burn out. Try to defuse the customer by listening to their complaint. Once you get off the phone, discuss the situation, if you can, with a co-worker or manager. Believe it or not, many business relationships are strengthened between clients and customers when they go through tough times together and don't give up on each other. Ideally, when customers stay with the client and make it through the tough times, this is when loyalty and bonding starts to develop between customers and clients. Valued clients usually don't forget who helped them through the tough times and in return they never leave.

MANAGERS:

Learning to respond and not to react has to come first from the leaders. If you are seen as the manager who slams the phone and reacts unprofessionally in the office, then you are not being a very good role model for your employees in the office. Your employee manual is not going to have every answer for every situation that your employees are going to encounter. As challenging events occur to your employees on the job, they are going to have to pull from something that they can relate to, in order to deal effectively with the situation. Untrained employees will usually emulate what they have seen in the office and will repeat phrases and responses that they have heard on the job under pressure to get them out of the "heat" of the situation. Employees will do this because that is what they assume is the right way to handle similar situations when under pressure and without prior experience in that situation. Because of this, make sure your employees have a positive role model. If you find yourself losing your temper close the door, call another manager, write negative thoughts down on paper (just don't send it to anyone) or get a glass of water. Most importantly remember not to react to the situation but to respond. Most business decisions don't have to be made immediately, take some time to evaluate the facts and then let the client or employee know that you will get back to them with an answer by a certain time. You wouldn't want your employees to lose their cool by reacting to clients, don't let them see their leader do it either.

"When we teach about anger, we help kids understand that it is almost always a secondary reaction and to look for what's underneath — are you hurt? Jealous? Our kids learn that you always have choices about how to respond to emotion, and the more ways you know to respond to an emotion, the richer your life can be."

Daniel Gorman, *Emotional Intelligence, p. 268, from the chapter, The ABC's of Emotional Intelligence.*

Lesson 18

Less is more, legally.

W HEN IT COMES TO E-MAILS AND LEGAL DOCUMENTS, LESS IS MORE. Here are the two most valuable rules of documentation:

Rule #1:
Don't put anything in writing that can be misinterpreted. Lawyers love this but business people don't. Always protect yourself from a legal battle or just from a misunderstanding that can sour a business deal by reviewing what you put in writing.

Rule #2:
Don't put anything in writing that you are unsure of. If you hesitate that the information is incorrect or outdated, don't ever put it in writing.

The less you put in writing, the less a person has to work with to misconstrue your intent. For example, if you don't know the answer to a question that is from an e-mail correspondence (since e-mail is a legitimate document) let the person know that it is a good question and that you will follow up with the answer ASAP. Do not guess an answer that you are unsure of. Instead, make a point of getting back to them or of referring them to someone else who would know the answer. This will protect you from legal battles down the road.

EMPLOYEES:

Always make sure that you are aware that people will use e-mails as proof of confirmation and as a legal document. Don't let any type of communication go out without proofreading your response and the material that you attach. If errors are found, it will reflect that you didn't take the time to pay attention to the details and that is not good for your reputation. Make sure you are always reading your e-mails and other forms of communication on a daily basis if possible. Save important documents to your server in a separate file. Any time that you receive a compliment for your services well done, print it out and save it for supportive reference material. Again, in reference to responding to questions or quotes by e-mail, make sure all of your correspondence is correct, since any errors can result in a legal problem. If you don't know the answer, don't guess an answer by putting it in writing. Get the correct answer or admit that you do not have the information necessary to supply the answer at that time. If you promise to follow up with client or co-worker, make sure you do follow up within a reasonable amount of time. By consistently following up on these promises, you will start to develop excellent follow up skills and will increase your understanding in the industry, all of which will help your career and your reputation.

MANAGERS:

When letters and e-mails are sent out to clients that are quotes for service, always have your employees send you the first copy before it goes out to make sure there are no errors in the content or spelling and that everything is included that is necessary to represent the line of business.

Since e-mail has become sometimes the main form of communication in many companies, it is imperative to make sure you are always reading e-mails on a daily basis. Make sure that your employees know how to work with e-mail and that they understand the features that are available in the application. You might be surprised to learn that some employees will know more than you about the application while others are scared to death to mention that they don't know anything at all. Always provide a review course for all of your employees on your e-mail system. Many times you will find out that many of the features that could enhance communication electronically are not being used because the employees and managers were never shown how to apply them. In summary, train your employees to proofread their forms of communication to insure all documents are clear, correct and not misleading. The time spent reviewing all correspondence from not being misconstrued will be worthwhile.

Lesson 19

Document changes and keep equal
communication between all parties.

W HEN CHANGES OCCUR DURING a business transaction, make sure everything is documented. Also be sure all of the parties involved in the transaction are updated. I learned this lesson the hard way from personal experience.

In 2002, I had a job order to fill on a temporary basis for a Fortune 500 company. The job was originally scheduled to last for 7-8 weeks for an administrative assistant position. The permanent employee was going out on medical leave and she had talked to me personally on the phone about the job specifics. She described the job to me and told me that she originally had planned to be out for 7-8 weeks for medical leave, but was just told by her doctor that she was now only going to be out for 3-4 weeks at the most. She had instructed me to find a person that could cover for her for 3-4 weeks. I found the temporary replacement and confirmed with HR verbally that the temporary staff member was available to take on the assignment. Everything was confirmed, verbally. On the first day of training, the temporary replacement was informed by the permanent administrative assistant that the assignment was to last for 7-8 weeks, not 3-4 weeks. The temporary staff member immediately called me to tell me that she could not commit to 7-8 weeks but only 3-4 weeks because she had a pending permanent job offer. A few minutes later, my contact in Human Resources called me to ask me why the temporary staff member was put in for 3-4 weeks, when it was a 7-8 week assignment. I told her that the permanent administrative assistant had told me personally on the phone that it was changed to a 3-4 week assignment. When my contact in Human Resources contacted the permanent administrative assistant, she denied that she told me 3-4 weeks. This put me in a very uncomfortable situation. **All of this was my fault because I failed to communicate with all the parties involved on the transaction (Human Resources, the permanent employee and the temporary staff member). If I had only communicated** with Human Resources and the permanent administrative assistant about the change in the job order time frame, all of this could have been prevented. This was a valuable lesson that I learned. I hope that you will also learn from this lesson.

EMPLOYEES:

Make sure at all times that all of your business deals are documented and well communicated to all parties involved. Use e-mail, conference calls, voicemails, letters, contracts, etc. Be sure to keep everyone informed. Don't leave anyone out and don't assume they don't need to know. Save all of your e-mails in an electronic or hard copy folder to refer to in reference to changes that were made along the way. This will prevent anyone from stating that they never received the information or a copy of the transaction. Be sure to still make follow up phone calls to go over everything before the deal takes place to eliminate any misunderstandings with all parties involved. This habit of consistently documenting and communicating with all parties at all times will consistently help to eliminate a lot of mistakes and misunderstandings with clients and co-workers and in return you will start to build a fine business reputation for being thorough.

MANAGERS:

As a manager please be aware that from time to time employees will forget or choose not to correspond with a contact because they just either did not have the time to communicate with the contact, didn't have the contact information, or they didn't think the contact needed to be informed. Whatever the reason, eliminate the chance of a business deal falling through by reinforcing with your employees that 100% correspondence is necessary on all business transactions with all parties involved, no exceptions. Make sure that all of your employees never assume the client does not need to know information. If it is relevant to their account, then they need to know.

Everyone needs to be reminded that all parties involved in a business transaction might not be consistently reading their e-mail, faxes or mail and that phone calls are just as important to ensure that every party involved in each business transaction is on the same page so no one drops the ball. It is always recommended to send an e-mail and follow up with a voicemail to insure delivery of the message.

Lesson 20

Pick your battles.

I PERSONALLY LEARNED THIS LESSON from my boss, Mark Christo, president/owner of the Monroe Group/Monroe Staffing Services. The lesson is about picking your battles.

Fact: On-the-job complaints about employees and managers are productive benefits of the job because they help to reinforce good behavior and identify bad behavior. Therefore complaints and compliments are an accepted part of running a successful business.

What can be unacceptable is when too many complaints come in from the same employee or employees on unrelated insignificant issues in a short amount of time. This is when the advice "pick your battles" comes in handy. If the complaint is not significant where it doesn't need to be addressed immediately, then don't address it. Make a note of the complaint but don't act on the complaint immediately if action does not need to take place. Instead, take care of the priorities that are on your desk. *Not every battle has to be fought.* There is not enough time in the day to address every issue, unless of course you are in the business of making money off receiving incoming complaints.

Admittedly, it can sometimes be a difficult task to decipher which complaints should be addressed immediately and which complaints should be ignored or at least not addressed as of yet. A good rule to help to identify the urgent complaints is to ask the following questions. (Please be aware there are certainly more questions to ask that are industry-specific and that these are only just a few to help to decide if the complaint should be dealt with immediately.)

- Does the complaint affect office morale?
- Does the complaint jeopardize current or future production of material or service?
- Does the complaint affect a person's health or safety?

- Does the complaint hold any consequences that could damage the company's reputation?
- Does the complaint reduce the company's level of customer service?
- Does the complaint affect any of the company's current or prospective clients?
- Does the complaint violate any laws?
- Does the complaint violate any environmental laws?
- Does the complaint give away any company confidential information to the competitors?
- Does the complaint conflict with the company, or an individual's, values or work ethics?

If the complaint generated a "yes" answer to any one of the above questions, then the complaint should be significant enough to be dealt with immediately. A good example of a "yes" answer would be if a person complained to management that the front walkway was slippery because of ice or snow. The manager should realize that the consequences of a person falling on the ice or snow, if he or she does not de-ice or shovel the walkway immediately, could be that an employee or visitor could slip, fall, injure themselves and sue the company for damages. That is a significant complaint. It is important to note that the manager is not the only person who should take action when a complaint is logged. Just because employees are at work doesn't mean they forgot what it means to make an environment safe and free of any potential liabilities.

If the complaint is a non-significant event, such as a person not keeping their desk as clean as possible or a person looking at an employee in an insulting way, then the matter can probably be addressed at a future time, if at all. Remember to "pick your battles" to make sure priority problems are dealt with first and many times the insignificant problems have a funny way of working themselves out.

EMPLOYEES:

A previous chapter discussed employees talking with their managers about small problems so they don't snowball into big ones. The problems that should be addressed should be business-related. If there is a personal problem that an employee is having with another co-worker then the two of them should at least try to work out that problem one on one before they go to the manager.

The first step to take when trying to work out the problem one on one is to make every effort of showing respect for each other and to understand each other's viewpoint.

Many times these differences can be worked out without involving the manager. All employees should be aware that managers don't like to have an employee complain all the time; it is exhausting to listen to especially during working hours when other business needs to be attended to. The old saying: "No one likes a complainer" is appropriate for this lesson. Please be aware that this lesson is not intended to make employees stop complaining, but it is just to request that they *evaluate the complaint to make sure it is valid.*

If you have ever worked with a person that is a constant complainer, then you know how exhausting it is to work with that person.

If you are that person that complains every day and no one has ever told you that your complaints bring them down yet, then do this test. The next time you are about to complain about something, get into the habit of asking yourself "is it significant?" Should you complain or should you not complain? One of my favorite authors of all time, Dale Carnegie *(How to Win Friends and Influence People)* is famous for one of his principles that states "don't condemn, criticize or complain." He suggests that a person should start with one day and try not to condemn, criticize or complain on or off the job. After the person successfully makes it through the one day, they are then encouraged to make it through a week without condemning, criticizing or complaining. If practiced enough, the person will start to see the uplifting, positive impact of not condemning, criticizing or complaining about insignificant events.

MANAGERS:

Fact: It is important to be aware and accept that employees will complain to each other on the job, by e-mail, at the water cooler, at night on the phone or in the office about company issues. Sometimes employees will even come to their managers to mention that "so and so" called me last night upset because of a shift change or job duty change, etc. A good bit of advice to follow in this case is *if the change that the manager has made has been communicated to all parties affected and accepted by the employee and the manager directly, then no other action needs to take place by the manager.* If the said employee is complaining about the change to other employees outside of the office, then the manager should just let it go and not address the issue. If it starts to affect the employee's morale, then the manager needs to address the issue. Otherwise there is no need for the manager to get involved until the employee comes directly to the manager to complain about a change. *It is important for managers to know that employees are allowed to complain and that they are allowed to vent their frustrations in response to change.* Change is inevitable; a manager could spend their entire day just dealing with insignificant complaints from employees. Instead, learn to "pick your battles" and teach your employees to do the same.

In summary, "picking your battles" doesn't mean avoid or ignore all complaints. It just means rationalize what needs to be addressed and what can be tabled or handled by the employees themselves, instead of in a formal setting. Realize that employees are entitled to complain to each other and that managers are *not to interfere* in every complaint between employees. Take the time to train your employees to learn to deal with diversity issues, and to understand where a person is coming from when there is a difference of opinion.

Fact: Understanding how to deal with diversity issues is a key characteristic to master in order to receive a promotion with many fortune 500 companies. Managers are not the only people who need to learn to get along with others. Make sure your employees know that their jobs depend on it too!

Lesson 21

Everything in Moderation

KEEPING EVERYTHING IN MODERATION is another one of life's rules that unfortunately many people seem to ignore. By ignoring the rule of "keeping everything in moderation," people will put themselves and others in harm's way by over-indulging in certain areas of their life, such as: drinking too much, eating in excess, or working too much.

When a person focuses too much of their attention on one thing, it is only natural for other areas of their life to become imbalanced or neglected such as family and spousal relationships, friendships, religious or spiritual guidance, personal health and fitness, education, financial stability, etc. What is suggested is to be conscious that the old adage does not lie "too much of a good thing is a waste." You should enjoy everything in life in moderation. You should never over-indulge in one specific area of your life. Instead, everything important in your life should be balanced meaning that you set aside specific time dedicated to each area that is important. If you have kids, you should have time set aside each day to bond with them and play with them. If you are married, time should be dedicated to your spouse, alone. If you own a house, time should be spent maintaining the home. As you can see, the list can continue until it becomes quite apparent that you have a lot of time to divide up. Just make sure the priority areas of your life, like your loved ones, get their well-deserved quality time first before anything. You will never regret that decision. Ask any person in a convalescent home what they wish they could have focused on more in life, the answer will be clear.

By following this old adage of keeping everything in moderation, you will feel great, look great, enjoy the time spent with loved ones, focus better on the job, receive great satisfaction in helping others and still enjoy the simple pleasures in life such as eating good food, and imbibing in great spirits, all without feeling guilty.

The following is a list of suggestions to consider to have a well balanced healthy life:

- Make it a priority to spend time with family and friends.
- Exercise in moderation, 3-4 times a week is enough.
- Volunteer your time in moderation.
- Drink plenty of water every day to stay healthy. A great tip to increase water consumption is to buy a case of water and keep it in your car for easy access to bring to work. When it is in your car you and your family will drink more water and less soda because it is easily available.
- Enjoy sweets or desserts but never in excess.
- Work in moderation, 40-45 hours a week is sufficient. If possible, try not to bring work home.
- Eat in moderation, always try to get into the habit of leaving the table content not overstuffed. At the first sign of fullness, put down the fork.
- Avoid taking antibiotics when at all possible.
- Buy and eat organically grown foods to reduce the amount of chemicals that go into your body on a daily basis.
- Watch TV in moderation; limit your viewing time to 1-3 hours a day, if that.
- Get out and spend time in nature, go for walks, or enjoy the beauty of your city or town. Travel to a nearby park.
- Round out your artistic appreciation by visiting museums or art galleries. Attend free concerts and/or plays.
- Go on vacations and by all means use your personal days. Those days are well earned and should be used to prevent burnout and allow you to take care of yourself.
- Do what makes you happy. Be sure to communicate to those who are near to you what you do need to do on a regular basis to be "happy with yourself." Examples could be to go to a movie by yourself, buy a cookbook and cook something you have never made before, buy a new CD, run in a road race, volunteer your time in a food kitchen or go to your local library. Whatever it is, make sure you find time to do what makes you happy. This will make you a happier person to be around because you did something that interested and benefited you.
- Drink alcoholic beverages in moderation; always know your limit.

Interestingly, none of these suggestions cost a significant amount of time or money for anyone to invest in, yet the rewards a person gains from spending the time to do them are incalculable. If a change in daily intake or if a health/fitness plan is in order, *do it today,* don't put it off another day!

If one of these suggestions has been a New Year's resolution over and over again, and has somehow never been created into a lifetime habit such as exercising 3-4 times a week for life, remember this: the body releases the same endorphins during sex as when working out. Knowing that you can have that natural good feeling within yourself at least three to four times a week is reward enough, isn't it? So get out there and just do it! No one ever mentioned that life was easy, but there are rewards for those of you who work hard during the process. These changes over time, if they are done in moderation will also help to increase a person's own confidence and and self esteem. A good friend of mine, Colette Pervais, once told me "if you form a positive or negative habit then the habit will form you." How true that statement is. Thank you, Colette.

In summation, everyone should spend time enjoying in moderation whatever makes him or her happy. They also need to allocate time on a weekly basis to balance out the important areas in their life that require their full attention in order to keep everything in working order. When certain projects take up more of your time than usual and other areas of your life suffer, make a point of finding time to rebalance the other areas quickly before problems start to occur.

EMPLOYEES:

From a health perspective, discipline yourself into a routine of working out 3-4 times a week on a regular basis for life no matter where you work or what you do for a living. Establish a routine to work out in the morning before work, during lunchtime or in the evening. Commit yourself to participate in an exercise schedule for the rest of your life to keep yourself healthy and to keep your stress level at a minimum. Remember stress is never going to go away. Learn to deal with it to stay healthy mentally and physically.

By exercising regularly, you will also reduce the number of sick days that you will have to take throughout the year. It pays to work out. It also costs in terms of your health if you don't. If you receive personal days and vacation days at work, make sure that you take them. It is extremely important to take a break from work from time to time to spend quality time with family and friends. You will always come back totally refreshed and rejuvenated. Try not to do anything in excess. When you leave work, try not to bring it home. Remember to keep all areas of your life in balance. The best advice I heard about this topic was from Jim Rohn, a well-known motivational speaker. For years in his seminars and tapes he has suggested something along the line of "when you are at work doing a specific task, focus 100% on that task and not on anything else. When you are in the shower, focus on the shower and nothing else, when you are with your family, focus on your family and nothing else." These words of advice from Jim Rohn can be applied to everything in life that you do. In return you will learn to pay attention to the important things in life and produce better outcomes.

MANAGERS:

It is a great idea to have companies pay for gym memberships for their employees. Did you know that according to an article in the *Daily News*, "1 in 8 workers will lose 5 hours of productivity due to a pain or condition. Companies lose more than $61 billion dollars a year due to headaches, backaches, toothaches and other torments." Don't you think that some of that money could have been saved if the companies encouraged their employees to work out every day and to see a dentist regularly?

Did you know that it is cheaper for companies to pay for gym memberships for their employees than to pay for the lost productivity time from employees that call in "sick" to cope with a "stress-related illness from on the job, stress or lack of exercise to increase their immune system?"

When companies make a decision to invest in their employee's health, they can choose to pay for new memberships to approved gyms or fitness centers in the area, reimburse current employees monthly membership dues or better yet have a gym built on site. It has been proven that this type of employee-sponsored program helps to reduce the amount of sick days with employees that do participate in regular exercise.

Company-sponsored gym memberships can also be an incentive to attract new employees or to maintain current employees.

Fact: When employees work out on a regular basis, even though they are taking time out of their regular work schedule, production never goes down. The only thing that goes down is their stress level, which will keep their immune system healthy and their sick day usage at a minimum.

As a manager, it is important to make sure that you lead by example by taking planned and approved personal days and vacations to demonstrate the importance of spending time on other interests. This is also a great time for your employees to take a break from your guidance temporarily and to prove to you that they are well trained and capable of running the office with little direction, thanks to your training.

Managers should also be the role models when it comes to regular exercise to show the importance of keeping stress at a minimum and to stay physically fit to demonstrate that they have self-control and discipline. Managers should always be encouraging their employees to do whatever it is that they need to do to reduce stress. Please note, for some employees it won't be a workout, so it is important not to push, but it is important that you at least pay attention to what they need to do to minimize their stress level, allow them to meditate, read, do yoga, sing, bowl, etc.

"You don't get stomach ulcers from what you eat, you get stomach ulcers from what is eating you." — Dr. Joseph Montague

Lesson 22

Understanding how people learn.

"People will generally accept facts as truth, only if the facts agree with what they already believe." — Andy Rooney

IT IS OFTEN SAID THAT TEACHERS usually make good sales people but has anyone ever investigated why that is? One suggestion could be that they have been taught to understand how people learn. Specifically, teachers learn in undergraduate school that there are six intelligences that are used to instruct a student on a lesson. The first is visual (eyes/seeing); the second is auditory (ears/hearing); third is kinesthetic/tactile (touch/feeling with your fingers); fourth is gustatory (tongue/taste); fifth is nasal (nose/smelling); and sixth is emotional (inter and intra personal skills/emotional aptitude).

The three primary intelligences that are used in persuasive business presentations or in effective employee training workshops are usually visual (charts), auditory (sounds, music, attention getters) and kinesthetic (samples of the products). The critical concept to understand in this chapter is to make business people realize that each client and employee learning style is different. Some people will only need to hear something in order to understand the material that is presented by a speaker to make a decision as to whether they want to buy or not. Some people who learn visually will need to read the information in a handout or on a board in order to "see" the meaning of the material. Kinesthetic learners will need to touch an example of something or maybe even relate to something else that is similar. In addition, always use a backup example of the concept in order to allow the audience to relate to a similar concept or idea in order to understand the point delivered.

When addressing an audience as a presentor, facilitator or trainer, it is important to be aware that everyone in the audience learns differently so the practical advice to follow would be to make sure you are utilizing at least the three primary intelligences every time information is delivered. The deliverable that is presented should be in writing for the visual learners to "see the point", it should be spoken clearly for the auditory learners to "hear what you are saying" and there should be a tangible item or example to represent the lesson for the kinesthetic people so they can "feel they understand" the lesson.

If you pay attention to commercials on TV, you will notice that marketing companies have paid attention to at least three of the 6 intelligences. The marketing companies are strategically ensuring that by targeting the three primary intelligences they can captivate the audience's attention no matter who is watching.

For example: A shampoo commercial will have an appealing spokesperson (visual), stimulating music (auditory) and some type of action dancing or putting shampoo in their hair (kinesthetic) to hopefully convince the viewing audience (at least the people that learn by visually, auditorilly or kinesthetically) to go out and buy the product.

In business, communication is essential; without proper communication everything breaks down. With the speed of business today, many business people are communicating business guidelines or suggestions and presentations in one form: email. This is a problem for the people who are kinesthetic and auditory learners. It is recommended when delivering key information in person: put it in writing, present it to them verbally and use examples to support the idea or lesson. This will help to reinforce that the lesson should be understood by whoever receives the information because you covered all your traditional learning pathways.

EMPLOYEES:

This lesson is valuable in all areas of business. When you start to talk to a person, you will be able to pick up after a conversation how a person learns if you pay attention to the words that they use to answer a basic question from the following example:

"Mr. Jones what is your interpretation of this idea that I just mentioned to you on the phone?"
(Reply)
"Mr. Smith I don't quite *see* what you mean, can you be a little *clearer?*"

It is obvious that Mr. Jones is a visual learner, the words that he is using to communicate is "see" and "clear". In order to get the point across to Mr. Jones, Mr. Smith will need to apply Mr. Smith's learning style, which would be to put something in writing so he can "see" it more clearly.

Does this make sense? What word would you use to tell the sales person you need more information?

If you are in sales and routinely conduct presentations to clients or employees, chances are you are already familiar with PowerPoint and its features. If you are not currently using PowerPoint or any other equivalent software, it is strongly suggested that you go buy it. Once you have installed the software and have learned the features, your presentations will be so much more exciting since you will now be able to incorporate sound, moving pictures and charts to captivate your audience and increase your audience's attention.

MANAGERS:

This lesson should be handed out to all of your employees, especially the employees that have to instruct or train others. Make sure that when new employees are being instructed on certain procedures that you are teaching the information using at least three of the intelligences. The hardest intelligence to apply would be the kinesthetic; when at all possible try to use an example so the kinesthetic people can at least relate the rule to something else that they are familiar with, especially if your product is intangible.

Earlier in the book, I mentioned to always use examples when instructing employees on new procedures and this specific lesson helps to support why it is important. There is a well-known assumption that new employees generally only absorb 30% of what they are taught during their first week on the job. This could be due to the new employee's attention span being blocked by anxiety, nervousness, fear, anger, intimidation and possibly depression. In addition they may be consumed with other thoughts that are related to their past job, nervous pressure from trying to impress their new co-workers or manager, or fearing that the job they are training for is too overwhelming for them at one time. A co-worker of mine once referred this emotional experience as "a case of the F.U.D.S." (Fear, Uncertainty, Doubts and Suspicions). As a manager or trainer to a new employee, please be aware that your employee will probably not absorb everything you train them on in the beginning. Because of this, the most important rules of the job should be taught several times, not just once and they should always be reinforced with examples verbally and in writing.

As a manager or trainer, aim to increase the absorption rate during training of new employees by using all three methods to help them train better. Use all three methods to help them to "understand", "feel" and "hear" or "see" the company rules, regulations and guidelines.

If you have employees presenting informational material to clients please review the following:

- Ensure they are equipped with the proper tools to create their materials (for example, use the latest software to capture the 4 different intelligences).
- Always train your employees on the "how to" procedures of trouble-shooting common hardware and software repairs in order to avoid embarrassing technical difficulties while they are out in the field.
- Observe your employee's presentation skills before they present formally to ensure they are persuasive during their presentations, make the best impression and that they know how to read and understand their audience.

Lesson 23

"Even if you are on the right track,
you get run over if you just sit there."
— Will Rogers

EVERYONE SHOULD CONSTANTLY LOOK for opportunities to improve or broaden their skills. One of the worst things a person can do is stay idle in the same position for 3-7 years. Many of the Fortune 500 companies train their recruiters to only hire candidates that are identified as "high potential". High potential candidates are employees that quickly move up in the ranks into positions of influence and authority. These candidates typically move or get promoted within 1-3 years in every position. They never stay idle in one spot. Does this sound like you? If the company you are working for does not promote that rapidly, then at least look for opportunities to take classes at a local college or to become part of a committee within the organization. By broadening your skills, you will be more marketable if and when the time comes to change jobs. Most companies would rather hire employees who choose to broaden their skills over a person who stayed idle and complacent in the same position. *Who Moved My Cheese?* by Spencer Johnson is a great book to read that makes readers aware of this topic. An example of improving a skill set would be learning new software even if you don't use it on the job currently. If you have a goal of switching careers to be, for example a graphic designer, try taking a class in Adobe Illustrator or Photoshop to at least familiarize yourself with the most popular applications in the marketplace. The most important day-to-day investment you can make with yourself to keep yourself motivated and marketable for tomorrow is to invest in yourself today with new ideas and skills. It is quite amazing what it will do just for your own self-esteem and attitude. That feeling is also very addictive so don't ever quit investing in yourself!

EMPLOYEES:

Keep yourself marketable by constantly taking advantage of any free training at work. You never know when a free certification course or a software course will come in handy in your next job. Don't ever take on the attitude that you have studied enough in your lifetime. You can never know enough. You also can never predict when you might be affected by a downsizing. Even the best employees are laid off from acquisitions and mergers, as well as bankruptcies. The more value you add to the company, the lower the odds that you will be the one to take the ax but if it does happen, at least it will increase your chances of being picked up rather quickly from a competitor.

MANAGERS:

Keep yourself marketable; middle management is often the area that gets laid off in downsizing cuts. In reference to your staff, keep the staff motivated by allowing them to attend seminars and classes that will make them more knowledgeable of the industry that they are in. This will also make them realize that you and the company believe they are worth investing money into for development and job security. Keep investing in yourself outside of work. Read the books that you find interesting even if they are not work related. Take up a hobby and master it; just like you do your job. Don't ever stop investing in yourself, your attitude deserves the investment. Everything else such as your motivation, leadership skills, enthusiasm and knowledge are all secondary to the benefits that you will gain by constantly investing time in attitude with self-development. It is contagious; don't let it get overlooked by laziness or self-doubt.

Lesson 24

Have a thirst for knowledge.

"Man's mind, once stretched by a new idea, never regains its original dimensions."
— Oliver Wendell Holmes

*"As for study, did not our wise teacher teach us that learning was of two kinds:
the one kind being the things we learned and knew, and the other being the
training that taught us how to find out what we did not know?"*
— George Clason, *The Richest Man in Babylon*

DON'T EVER STOP LEARNING. Just because you have completed a milestone in your education by graduating from high school, college, graduate school, medical school or technical school, it does not mean that you will never open up another book or take another course. On the contrary, what lies ahead of you is to find the diamonds in the rough and navigate your way through life using your own interests and people that you associate with as a class course selection guide. The people you meet and spend quality time with will suggest books to read that will give you a heightened awareness of a subject matter that you want to know more about or that someone has identified that you need to know more about.

If you can't continue your education through a university or a college program, then read as many magazines, books, journals and newspapers that you can get your hands on. I encourage you to listen to as many audiotapes and motivational CD's in the car while commuting to work as possible to keep your motivation high and to constantly be educating yourself with new ideas and perspectives. Remember your public libraries are free, so there is no excuse why you cannot obtain material to read. It is also wise to increase your knowledge of other industries to enhance your knowledge base so that you can intelligently speak to other people from other industries about their interests and challenges. A great networking opportunity is to swap business books with clients. This will always give you a reason to visit a client or prospective client at least once a month to swap books, share ideas and/or maintain business and increase your knowledge of other industries.

Again, these conversations will always give new insight on similarities and differences that may help solve a situation in your job or just make you realize that everyone can teach you something you can learn from.

EMPLOYEES:

Read trade journals/magazines, books, newspapers, and free email newsletters. Ask co-workers and managers what you should be reading to stay informed in the current marketplace. Join a local chapter of trade representatives in your industry. This will allow you to stay up-to-date with current trends in the industry. Interact with other business professionals to increase your knowledge of the community and how others are affected by changing conditions in the economy.

MANAGERS:

Pass your trade journals/magazines, favorite books, newsletters and informative emails on to your employees. They will be flattered that you care enough to keep them up-to-date with the industry trends. To ensure that the employees read it, ask for the employees to sign the handout or magazine once they have read it and then have them return it to your desk when done to give you feedback on the information they just read.

"No one is as smart as everyone." — Larry Keely

"If we all believed in the same thing, there would be no such thing as gambling."
— unknown

Life Lesson 4

Goals; create memories not regrets.

I HAVE ALWAYS BEEN ONE to set New Year's resolutions and my favorite resolution was to run the NYC marathon. I ran the marathon at 33 years old, in 11/2001, and did it in a non-record breaking 4½ hours. The reason why I share this personal experience with you is to show you that anyone can accomplish what they set out to do, *if they don't give up and if they don't let anyone else stop them.* I recall often that when I shared my goal about wanting to run the NYC Marathon with someone, they would come back with a reply like "why would you want to do a thing like that?" or "Lisa, you are never going to make it, do you know how long 26.2 miles is?" Does this sound familiar? At that moment, I realized why so many people don't accomplish their goals. *It wasn't because they failed to communicate their goals to other people or that they didn't want to accomplish the goals they set. Instead, it was because they let other people talk them out of being motivated to want to accomplish the goal.* Specifically, they would allow the negative reinforcement from friends and colleagues such as "you will never do it" or "why would you want to do that?" to influence their goal setting motivation and commitment. As a result, the goal is questioned, put off and is never accomplished. Does this sound familiar?

The learning lesson here is that a person should never let others intimidate/influence them to abandon their goal. It is their goal, not anyone else's. Everyone should live their life to the fullest. They should do what they are meant to do on this earth. No one else is like them, that is what makes them special. They should follow their dreams to do what it is they are guided to do on this earth. If they need to, they should find a group of people that have a common interest in a similar goal and meet with them on a regular basis to keep them in pursuit of their goal. Trust me, once a person proves to themself that they can accomplish a goal, all the rest of their goals they set for a lifetime become attainable. When a person truly believes in their goal(s), they will not let any obstacle (person/thing) deter them from reaching their goal.

On a personal note, this is why I ran the marathon; because it helped to reinforce in me that I could accomplish anything I wanted to as long as I believed in myself and stopped worrying about what other people think of me and my goals.

Consequently, after I finished the NYC Marathon, my husband said to me, "Thank goodness you accomplished your life goal. Now we can go back to living a normal life." I turned to him and said, "Honey, I hate to tell you this but this was just the beginning, all the rest of my goals seem to be a little more attainable now. If I can do this I can do anything." I started this book 2 months later after contemplating writing it for 10 years.

"I think what I represent is achieving what you want in life. It's a matter of attitude. Some people have a negative attitude, and that's their disability."
— Marla Runyan

Legally blind Marla Runyan ran the NYC Marathon in 2002 and finished in fifth place for women at 2:27:10.

Lesson 25

When setting a goal, make sure everyone knows what is required to accomplish the goal.

D ID YOU KNOW THAT MILLIONS of employees go to work every day for years never knowing what the company's current or future goals are? Are you one of them? Are you involved in accomplishing those corporate goals? Have you ever been involved in accomplishing a company goal? Do you know what your company goal is this year? Did your company accomplish its goal from last year?

It is the CEO or president's responsibility to make sure that a company goal is set forth every year for the entire company to be aware of and to follow. The message or goal should be clear and attainable. Many companies, unfortunately, have forgotten to set or communicate their company goal(s) to all of their employees. Often times the sales department is given monthly or quarterly goals but the rest of the company just goes about their days, months and years never knowing where the company wants to go. Other companies have simply forgotten to update their current goal or to adjust them accordingly to the current economy.

Fact: Everyone in the company from the receptionist to the accounting department and the sales department should be kept abreast of what the overall company objective or goal is for the quarter or the year. Everyone should also be entitled to view the current status by either reading a memo, website or bulletin that will give all employees an overview as to how the company is doing currently. This will help to ensure that every employee feels as if they are part of a team contributing to the goal, which will hopefully cause them to feel more informed, focused and motivated.

Eventually, as production and service starts to increase to the meet the company goal, employees will start to get a tangible feeling or idea of what it takes personally to contribute to accomplishing a company goal. Once the goal has been hit, management needs to ensure that everyone is appreciated and/or rewarded. The reward can be as simple as a letter of achievement, a broadcasted e-mail, a bonus or a company party. The extra effort that is invested in thanking employees and managers for a job well done accomplishing the company's goal will go a long way in reference to employee satisfaction. At this point it is also critical to reset the goal to the next level so that the pace continues to increase and business grows.

There is another goal that is not the company's responsibility and that is a personal goal that should be set by each employee every year.

Every year each employee (and manager) should write down what it is that they want to accomplish for that year. The goal could be to get a promotion, learn a new computer application, grow the business by 30%, attend more charity functions or to network more. The goal should be a goal that, once achieved, should increase an employee's worth, self-confidence, work life balance or skill set. Generally, once the goal has been set, the employee should share the goal with managers, co-workers and family, so that a support system is in place to help to reinforce the goal.

Employees should write down the mini-steps that are necessary to accomplish their goal. If the goal is to learn Spanish by taking classes at night then the employee should start by signing up for a Spanish course at night for beginners and then to plan out the following semesters with the intermediate and advanced classes in mind to continue the educational goal. This habit of setting and accomplishing a yearly goal will create a lifelong habit of constant achievement. The end result will be an employee that is motivated, driven and confident.

Start today by creating a lifelong habit of setting personal goals on a yearly basis.

In reference to the personal goal, employees should be instructed not to set the personal goal so high that they can't attain it. That would just be self-defeating. If the goal is to make more money and let's say the employee is currently making $45K, then instead of setting a goal to make $100K, the employee should create mini steps and start with making first $60K, then $80K and so on. Many people set goals that are just too unrealistic. Once the year is over and they didn't accomplish their goals, they think that "it just isn't in the cards for them to reach that goal." In reality, all they needed to do was take mini- steps to get there. By taking the mini-steps to accomplish their goal, they would have reinforced in themselves along the way that they can accomplish anything they want to do which would have kept them on track with their goal! By taking the mini-steps it also gives a person an idea of what it feels like to keep that level of accomplishment alive. Through the journey of accomplishing the mini-steps they start to learn what it takes to consistently achieve that level of success and also what it requires in sacrifice of personal time to keep the momentum and motivation going to continue to surpass that goal and to set higher goals.

All goals should be written down with steps detailing how the goal will get accomplished. The reward should also be included to keep the focus and motivation in clear sight. Be sure to take the time to acknowledge your accomplishment's along the way with small rewards. It is very important to feel that sense of accomplishment for a job well done.

I recall a statement that was repeated over and over from a friend of mine, Dr. Robert Carrow, of the Visionary Foundation while I was training for my first marathon that relates to this lesson of setting goals. Dr. Carrow would constantly state to me, "Lisa, enjoy the journey of who you become while training for the marathon because it is who you become while training that is the biggest reward of all, not the fact that you ran a marathon." At first I did not see the value in the statement, but once I started the training by waking up at 5:30 AM every morning to fit in the short runs and committing hours on the weekend to complete the long runs, it started to make more sense to me. After completing every run that I did, I was noticing that I would receive reinforcement from myself that I can do whatever I set my mind to because I just finished a run that I was not sure I felt I could accomplish or felt like doing at that time. Interestingly, at the end of every run usually an hour later or so my thoughts would already be thinking about the next run. *The closer I got to the actual marathon day, the stronger my confidence grew because I had built up so much reinforcement from my previous runs. I had created an attitude that was now ingrained in me that I could do anything I set my mind to.*

I shared this personal experience with you to help to reinforce in all of you that the rewards you receive from going after your goals are priceless. No amount of money in the world can buy you confidence in yourself. *You have to earn that the hard way, one accomplishment at a time.* So let's get started today. If you have not set a goal for this year, personal or career, set it, write it down, post it where you can see it every day and start working towards it. The benefits from setting and accomplishing a goal are a reward in itself because it just sets you up for constant achievement in whatever you do.

EMPLOYEES:

If your manager has not communicated the company goal to you, please inquire about it so that you are clear on the company's goal. Request that the manager set up a personal goal to accomplish in the next year. Make sure the manager shows you how to get there and gives you examples of what is expected. Ask what the manager will do for you once you reach that goal and get it in writing. Put that goal on your desk so that you can visually see the goal every day. Be sure to touch base with the manager if you see any signs of struggle working towards that goal. Believe in yourself that you can accomplish the goal but making sure you have all the necessary training to meet the goal. Remember to enjoy "who you become" while working towards that goal because it is just as important as reaching that goal and many times more important.

MANAGERS:

Sit down with your employees and let them know what you expect of them. Show your employees which direction the company is going. Write down the company goal and the employee's personal goal. Managers will often make the mistake of throwing out a goal for an employee to follow as a target goal but unfortunately they don't tell the employee how to get there. Make sure you spend the time to set a realistic goal and show your employees what they need to do to attain that goal. Make sure the employee is completely trained to perform all actions that are necessary to accomplish the goal. If they are not, take the necessary time immediately to get the employee trained ASAP.

A good suggestion to help to reinforce goal setting is to create a "daily task sheet for success" for your employees to fill out. This sheet requires an employee to write their goal on a daily basis, which is simply excellent reinforcement. On the top of this sheet they are required to write out their top tasks that they need to get accomplished for the day. There is also a daily time schedule on the corner of the sheet that they can use to set up their schedule to manage their time effectively, such as doing like things together. For many employees, time management does not seem that important and it is often not given a second thought because the employees don't yet relate to its value. The best advice that can be shared with that issue as a manager is to keep being an excellent role model by managing *your* time effectively. Eventually the top performers will relate and follow your lead and the ones that don't won't.

Getting back to the daily task sheet, the top of the document required the employee to put their name, the date, their personal goal and three tasks they need to complete for the day to get closer to their goal. Would you believe that an office of mine filled these daily task sheets out faithfully every day for three months and that every one of my employees, as well as myself, hit their own personal goal and the office goal for that quarter! I credit the success of this daily task sheet to the fact that it forced the employee to write down their own personal goal every day by putting mini-tasks as to how to get there. At the end of the day, they were able to see they completed the mini-tasks, which gave them a small sense of personal accomplishment and got them one step closer to their goal. This small sense of personal accomplishment is absolutely necessary to instill in employees, especially employees who might be new to goal setting. Managers should always be aware of the goal setting rule that the employees first need to be shown specific examples as to how to attain the goal. Role models or examples should be used if available. Specific guidance is necessary for a successful journey towards accomplishing a goal! Don't be the type of manager that just throws a goal out and then shuts the door until the deadline is up. The end result will be that you will just be setting yourself up for disappointment in yourself and your staff.

Once the personal goals have been met, they should be acknowledged, rewarded and reset. This increases the employee's professional development, focus and motivation on the job.

The daily task sheet can be of value to the manager also, if they collect them and evaluate them at the end of the day. This is because the manager is able to view each employee's daily activity and is reminded of each employee goal. In addition, at the bottom of the sheet there is an area that asks the employee to write down what they learned from the day's activities. There is another question that asks for the employee to grade themselves on their production level from 1-5, 5 being the best. This information, if filled out regularly, will give a manager insight as to what is going on personally with each employee. It will give them information that might not usually be conveyed throughout the business day that can be constructive or destructive to the office environment. These comments will help the manager to keep a pulse on the office morale. The comment topics can and should vary from situations that occur on the job, to troubleshooting situations on the computer or with human relations skills training. All of the comments are great reference sources to bring up discretely during employee meetings. The information presented will hopefully help to guide an employee to deal with a current situation that they have not yet been trained to handle in a more professional manner or at least give them something to use as a guide. With the speed of business today it is obvious that many employees are not trained as well as they could be. These informal meetings discussing the topics from the sheets help to round out an employee's training by usually talking about the material or situation in an informal setting at a time when the employee is able to relate to the training. Encourage your employees to fill out a similar sheet; the rewards will be mutually beneficial. Managers should also fill out a sheet on a daily basis as well!

"Success is the continuous journey toward predetermined worthwhile goals."
— unknown

A copy of the "Daily Task Sheet For Success"
can be downloaded from
www.gumptiontraining.com

Lesson 26

*Success only occurs when you
turn a dream into reality.*

ONCE YOU HAVE IDENTIFIED your dream or goal that you want to pursue and you accept that no one is going to influence you not to go after your goal, then begin with mini-steps. Create an action plan that is composed of several mini steps to get you on the right track to your goal. Remember, if you don't take action, then nothing is going to change. Don't be one of those people who has the dream in their head but never follows through.

Start by telling selected people about your goals, the people that won't sabotage your goal (remember: it is your goal, not theirs). Write down the goal in a journal. Create a plan on how to accomplish the goal. List people you know who might guide you in the right direction and then contact them for advice as to how to get started. It is not recommended to quit your current job when you realize that action needs to take place but at least get yourself closer to the goal by creating an action plan that is realistic and attainable.

If it is a business you want to open, then take a "small business" class, learn to write a business plan or start to look at how the business could get funded. Talk to someone that already has a similar business and find out the do's and don'ts of the business by asking the right questions. If you don't take action with your career, then it is not going to magically appear. Take control of your career before someone else has control of it!

Are you in your dream job? No? What is your dream job? Write it down. Do you not know what to do with your life? A good book to read is *What Color is Your Parachute?* (The 2002 edition by Richard Bolles.) If you have read the book and are still confused, here is a quick 5-minute career evaluation you can do on yourself. I created this myself as an interviewing and career guidance tool to use when my clients didn't know what they want to do as a career. This exercise uncovers values and beliefs from childhood, which I firmly believe have the real connection to a person's career interest.

Please take the next five minutes to complete this exercise. If you are unhappy in your current position and don't understand why, then this exercise might reveal what you are missing and/or what you need that is not being fulfilled in your career.

When you do this exercise please be honest with your answers, you will only be lying to yourself if you don't answer honestly. With each question write down at each age stage of life what you wanted to be when you grew up and why? For example, these are my answers to the following career questions:

"*When I was 5 years old,* I wanted to be a nurse because I wanted to *help people* by making them healthy."

"*When I was 10 years old,* I wanted to be an author because I liked to write about things that would *help people* and influence people."

"*When I was 16 years old,* I wanted to be a US Senator because I wanted to speak in front of people and make changes to the world to *help* make it a better place."

"*When I was 21 years old,* I wanted to be a doctor because I wanted to *help people* feel better mentally and physically."

When I evaluate all the reasons why I was motivated to do a specific career at a certain time in my life, I have one main repeating focus and that was to help people. While growing up I was choosing different role models and careers based on belief systems that I was developing as a result of interpretations from positive or negative events in my life. This is normal. The job titles changed but the repeating focus stayed the same, I wanted to help people in many different ways verbally, legally/politically, physically and mentally. When I look at what I became, it all makes sense. I received a degree in biology because I was very interested in understanding the human body in order to stay healthy and to encourage others to stay healthy. I am a recruiter who helps people to find employment and I am also a manager who helps to instruct and coach people to learn how to succeed. I am also a writer who has shared my knowledge and experiences with the world. My career path has literally embraced all of my childhood interests at each stage of my life, which has helped to develop my beliefs, values and interests. *I am happy in my career currently because I am able to tap into my inner interests on the job.* If your job does not allow you to tap into your inner interests, then stimulate that interest through a hobby or on a volunteer basis. Your inner interests play a vital role in who you are and your level of happiness. Don't let your interests remain idle because a part of you will feel unfulfilled.

Please do this exercise right now. If you are unhappy with your job, you might just realize that it is not the right match for you based on inner interests that are not being fulfilled or met. There are millions of people who simply chose a career because of someone else's influence (a parent or relative); many people will now realize that their career is now probably not the best match for their interests or personality any longer. Maybe this exercise will be the motivating factor you have been waiting for to make a change.

On a separate sheet of paper, write out the following questions leaving space to write the answer after each question.

- At age 5 years old: what was your career goal and why?
- At age 10, what was your career goal and why?
- At age 16, what was your career goal and why?
- At age 21, what was your career goal and why?

Is there a repeating interest? Many times this might bring up some bad memories. If these memories have not been resolved, then it might be a good time to revisit these feelings and change a belief system that a person might have about an experience or memory. This might be why a person is not happy in their current job, due to an unresolved childhood experience. A true example of this would be: A man might realize that at 16 years of age he wanted to be a policeman to help people because he witnessed his powerless mother being abused by his father. Maybe he never became a policeman because he always felt powerless due to his father's influence on him. If this man never sought out any counseling to work through these feelings then there is a good chance he might have some anger or resentment that needs to be resolved or confronted. It would definitely be wise that he should seek support from a licensed therapist to change some old beliefs that are limiting his abilities. (Please be aware that this is not a sign of weakness; instead, it is a sign that the person chooses to be stronger.) Once this man accepts the past and is able to release any unresolved issues from childhood, he just might be able to go after the job of his dreams without any conscious or unconscious feelings of insecurity that would cause him not to pursue his goal of becoming a police officer.

"A chain is only as strong as its weakest link." — C. Kingsley

Many people, after completing this exercise, are going to realize they chose the wrong career for one reason or another. In reality, their personality and interests actually match up to a completely different career path. A good example is when an accountant identifies that he has a strong creative interest from childhood and now he finally realizes the reason why he is dissatisfied in his job is not because he is not good at what he does, instead it is because it does not have a creative outlet for him. In order for the accountant with a creative interest to be happy on the job, he will need to exercise his creativity by either assuming some creative responsibilities, or by doing something creative outside of work. If he wants to make a career change altogether, then he could start by maybe getting a degree in marketing and then switch his career to marketing. Maybe he could handle marketing for accountants? He would have the best of both worlds.

EMPLOYEES:

I encourage all of you to evaluate your current job. Evaluate what your level of job satisfaction is. Are you excited to go to work every day? What do you like about the job? What gets you in the "work zone"? (Work zone = when an employee is doing what they like to do on the job.)

Many career professionals state that employees only get in the work zone 30% of the day; the other 70% is spent doing repetitive mundane tasks. Employees would be much more productive if they could figure out a way to make sure they were in the zone more often. By placing employees in the zone more often, productivity would increase and so would profits.

The solution is: employees need to learn to delegate mundane tasks to a support person in the office when at all possible. If this is not possible, employees should at least try to manage their time more effectively by always making sure that "like things are done together" to conserve time and to increase the amount of time spent in the zone.

An example of this is Susan, a marketing assistant who enjoys being in the zone by putting together client deliverables (presentations, graphs, pie charts, manuals, brochures, etc). Susan is also responsible for doing research, data entry and filing, which she finds boring. If Susan effectively managed her time by completing "like things together" she would reduce the amount of time that she spends handling the boring tasks. When she does each task separately, with little or no interruption, the tasks will be done quicker and more productively since there was little distraction from the task at hand. This causes an employee to be very efficient because they are concentrating on just one task at a time. Once Susan completed the filing, research and data entry work, again with no interruptions, then the rest of the day could be spent creating the client deliverables allowing her to focus 100% on what she likes to do best by being in the zone. Susan is likely to not lose her concentration while in the zone because all the remedial tasks that would break her concentration have been completed.

To increase the time spent in the zone, an employee will probably need to increase their workload. Realistically speaking, the normal job description will not substantiate an employee to be in the zone 100% of the time, due to budget constraints and manpower shortage. When an employee identifies what their zone is, they should at least communicate to management what they like to be responsible for while on the job and to request that they receive any extra work related to that responsibility from other staff members. It would also be a good idea to suggest to management to try to find out if there is anyone in the company who has a preference for research work or data entry or filing, which would eliminate the mundane tasks and increase the workload for someone that likes to be in the zone by handling filing or doing data entry. You should tell management that you are still willing to handle your current responsibilities but want to make them aware of your career interests and that any additional responsibilities toward your interests would be appreciated.

MANAGERS:

It is just as important to make sure that managers are in the right job. If after completing the exercise on the previous page you then realize that being a manager is not what you want to do, then start to take action. Begin by looking at other positions within your organization that you can advance to. If you are convinced that a management position is for you but you currently go home every night stressed out about the day's activities or about poor performance of your current employees, then you should do something about it. Either increase your employees' production by spending more time training them or sit down and find out what they need to do to increase their production level. Most often, your employees will already have the answer, they just need to hear it from up above.

At the very least you must understand the business that you are in, understand the cost of doing business, the cash flow situation and the peaks and valleys in supply and demand. Once a manager understands why budgetary decisions are made, it often becomes clearer for a manager to effectively manage.

In reference to the employees, always investigate what you can do to help your employees to be in the zone more often than 30% of the time. Restructure the office if you have to, redistribute job tasks or bring in additional support staff. The benefit of listening to the needs of your employees is priceless. They will be grateful that you spent the time to learn more about them and their interests. Even if the office cannot hire more staff to handle the tasks that are not favored, at least the office will run more efficiently once they learn to complete "like things together" to be more productive.

For example: Bakers know the value of doing like things together, by making one type of cookie at a time. A baker when preparing to gather the ingredients for 2 large separate cookie orders follows the lesson correctly of doing like things together. The baker will prepare and bake all the same type of cookies at one time. Never would he choose to prepare and bake only 1 dozen sugar cookies to then move on to preparing and baking 1 dozen peanut butter cookies and then back to preparing and baking 1 dozen sugar cookies to complete the order. That would waste valuable prep, production and cleanup time. This example should hopefully demonstrate the value of disciplining yourself to do like things together to increase production and quality output on a routine basis.

Lesson 27

Life is too short to be insecure.

"Always be you and not like anyone else, because nobody ever wants a counterfeit bill." — unknown

IF YOU HAVE NEVER HAD A PROBLEM with being insecure in any area of your life, then please go on to the next chapter. If you have experienced insecurity in some area of your life, then please read on.

The feeling of insecurity is one of the most exhausting feelings in the world. It can stunt a person's growth, self-development and self-worth. Whether it is about your appearance, body image, career choices, family or current financial situation; whatever it is, stop the senseless self sabotage! Please accept that no one in this world is perfect and that is what makes the world so interesting. The adversity that people have had to overcome with their insecurities is what makes them a respected role model for others to be motivated by.

Millions of successful people can vouch that an individual's weakness can blossom into their strength if they acknowledge it, stop limiting themselves with it and take the steps to overcome it today. This is not something you will want to put off until tomorrow.

According to several studies conducted over the years it is estimated that millions of people in the population today have some type of insecurity based on an event or series of events that occurred during childhood. These events often relate to being exposed to violent behavior from parents, grandparents, siblings or other people in the community. Typical abuses that millions of people have never sought help from would be from verbal, physical or mental abuse, betrayal and/or the loss of a loved one. These same people must be aware that if they did not seek therapy for the event(s) after it happened and instead suppressed it, that the emotions suppressed are highly likely to emerge later on in their adult life. Through my own experiences, I have learned two significant facts about this subject:

1) It is never too late to address an issue that has caused some type of insecurity in a person.

2) It is never too late to deal with an event, reinterpret the event and liberate one's self from that insecurity.

Sadly, there are millions of adults today that are still going through the motions with some type of insecurity based on a childhood event(s). It is also painstaking to see a person think or react a certain way all because of something that happened years ago. If this is happening to you, please try to reconcile that insecurity, it will be an amazing breakthrough in your business and private life if you do.

Dr. John Gray, well-known author of *Men are from Mars, Women are from Venus,* touches on this topic in the following paragraph:

"Many people grow up too quickly because they reject and suppress their feelings. Their unresolved emotional pain is waiting inside to come out to be loved and healed. Although they may attempt to suppress these feelings, the pain and unhappiness continue to affect them."

Dr. John Gray, *Men are from Mars, Women are from Venus,* p. 240.

The following example is my own personal experience with this subject matter. It is in reference to a childhood insecurity that matured into my adult life on and off the job. In order to effectively communicate this lesson I need to reveal personal information that is going to be stated about my father, Joseph J. Connolly III. He was diagnosed with manic depression in his early twenties which caused him to have mood swings, erratic behavior patterns, psychiatric treatments, hospitalizations, etc. He never hurt me in any way except that I felt embarrassed for myself and him because of his random manic episodes. To say the least he was very different from all the other fathers.

I grew up never wanting to emulate him in any way because at the time I did not understand that manic depression was a "disease" that could be difficult to control for some people such as my father. As I was growing up, I strived to always look "successful" since I interpreted my father as being "unsuccessful". (Please note that this was just my "interpretation" of this event as a child.) Otherwise, I had a great childhood. My father retired from the military after serving 20 years and our family moved to Cheshire, Connecticut. I attended high school, played sports and worked a part-time job at a dry cleaners throughout high school. After graduation, I attended Keene State College, in New Hampshire for three years. I then transferred to Southern Connecticut State University and earned a degree in Biology. Once I graduated, I started my career in recruiting, married, bought a house and had two children.

It wasn't until I was 29 years old that I learned about my subconscious insecurity/value that had emerged from my childhood, in reference to my father. It was during the winter of 2000 when my good friend Emily Williams offered me two tickets to attend a self-development seminar in Orlando, Florida. The event focused on self-development, specifically by understanding personal values, self awareness, understanding why you are the way you are, etc. Out of curiosity, I accepted the tickets and went with my husband, George, to the 5-day event. We booked our flights, arranged for daycare, packed our bags and headed down to Florida with no idea what was about to unfold.

A few days into the seminar, I was required to write down my inner-most values in order of importance. My list started off like this:

1) Success
2) Health
3) Family
4) Love
5) Trust
6) Security
7) Friendship

The next step of the exercise was to identify what event in my life influenced me to hold these values so high in that specific order of importance? This is when the exercise changed my life! Up until that moment, I never realized that I had created such a "crutch" by putting "success" ahead of my "family" value, all because I was embarrassed of my father while growing up. To that day, I was still striving for success as my primary motivation in life and was putting family, love and friendship secondary. Fortunately, through the help of this seminar, I learned that I needed to address this issue or else I would spend the rest of my life putting "success" ahead of my family. What a shocking revelation! The following day at the seminar was spent learning how to address the issue. In my case, it was awkward but simple. I had to get on the phone with my father, let him know why I felt this insecurity and then apologize to him for being embarrassed of him. Needless to say, it was a courageous act that paid off for him and I.

Thankfully, because of this exercise, I have rid myself of a childhood insecurity that was guiding me in the wrong direction as an adult. Consequently, I now have a better relationship with my father than ever before. No longer am I embarrassed of my father; in fact, I find a lot of humor in many of his manic episodes. I only regret that I wasn't mature enough to laugh at half of those episodes as a child when they happened. I love you, Dad, just the way you are!

Words cannot effectively express how powerful this exercise can be for anyone. Please take the time to evaluate your current values in order of importance and then identify why you choose those values in that order? You might notice after you have participated in this exercise that your values will be right on target, shift a bit or change completely. Please be aware that this exercise might involve a few tears, so don't hesitate to consult a licensed therapist, if necessary.

On a personal note, I shared this experience with all of you so that you may all benefit emotionally as I did. It is important to accept that many of us have obstacles (interpretations/unresolved issues/insecurities) still to over-come from our childhood. Some use those obstacles as a crutch to bring them down which subconsciously causes them to never get where they want to be in life. Others overcome those same obstacles and use that liberation as a spring board to launch them up to their fullest potential in life. It is your decision to make. In reference to your fullest potential, are you going to use your obstacles as a crutch or a springboard?

Here are some words for thought by Daniel Goleman, author of *Emotional Intelligence and Destiny.*

"Much evidence testifies that people who are emotionally adept who know and manage their own feelings well, and who read and deal effectively with other people's feelings are at an advantage in any domain of life, whether romance and intimate relationships or picking up the unspoken rules that govern success in organizational politics. People with well-developed emotional skills are also more likely to be content and effective in their lives, mastering the habits of mind that foster their own productivity; people who cannot marshal some control over their emotional life fight inner battles that sabotage their ability for focused work and clear thought." (Emotional Intelligence, Daniel Goleman, pg. 36, part 2, *Emotional Intelligence and Destiny,* by Bantam Books, 1995.)

EMPLOYEES:

This advice is mostly on a personal level but it is important to realize that it does affect how you work and how you relate to other people. If you are thinking about getting married or having a family, please do this exercise, it may help to eliminate irreconcilable differences before they start.

It is certainly hard enough to change a habit or insecurity when you are aware of it, but if you go your entire life never even evaluating your values, then you have done a disservice to yourself and the ones you love. Many times people have negative habits or values and don't even know why they have them. This exercise might just reveal those reasons just in time to be able to liberate your self from them and save you a lifetime of regret.

For example, a common bad habit that some people have is to treat other people rudely with no justification. If you are a person that unjustly treats a person badly or rudely for no reason then this chapter will do wonders for you. Try working on why you feel the need to be rude to people. I guarantee if you probe hard enough you will reveal an unresolved issue that needs to be addressed.

MANAGERS:

As a manager, it is just as important to be aware of what your insecurities are and why you have them. Are you sending the right message to your employees carrying that insecurity? Are you presenting the best values to your employees? Definitely consider doing this exercise because you might be able to change, rearrange or delete a value that might be confusing your employees or guiding them in the wrong direction. Don't ever consider exercises like this as a sign of weakness. It's just the opposite.

Just imagine if every one of your employees completed an exercise like this one, how powerful your staff would be with very few crutches to hold them back, in reference to their performance. What this exercise can do in a few minutes can save human resources departments thousands of dollars in performance development consulting, seminars and self improvement courses. Imagine if everyone in the world completed this exercise, what a peaceful world it would be.

I do recommend that everyone should repeat this exercise every few years to check in with themselves. This regular check up will help to make sure there are no negative influences guiding a person on the wrong track. It is expected that as people grow their values change based on what is going on in their life at the time. This exercise is especially helpful with married couples to better understand each others needs as they mature. (I recommend once a year that married couples sit down and do this exercise together to strengthen themselves and their relationship.)

"The most exhausting thing in life is being insecure."
— Anne Marrow Lingbery

"Most physical diseases are now widely accepted as being directly related to our unresolved emotional pain. Suppressed emotional pain generally becomes physical pain or sickness and can cause premature death. In addition, most of our destructive compulsions, obsessions and addictions are expressions of our inner emotional wounds."

— Dr. John Gray, *Men are from Mars, Women are from Venus,* p. 240.

Life Lesson #5

*Adversity, take the high road and
let others benefit from your experience.*

M Y HUSBAND AND I TOOK A COUPLE, Sally and John (names changed) out to dinner during the summer of 2002 to thank them for helping my husband land a new job. During dinner, Sally had mentioned that she had recently inherited her father's entire estate, which included a house and a small trust fund. I asked her if she had any relatives that were also heirs to his estate. She told me that originally, the will was equally distributed but in the last days of her father's life it was changed, unbeknownst to her. Earlier that year, her father had fallen ill and Sally was the only person that took care of him in his final dying days. No one else in her family bothered to care for him. Without her knowledge, her father changed his will from equally distributing the estate amongst Sally and her brother, to making Sally the sole heir. He did this because throughout his entire life he admitted to himself — and to Sally in the will — that he never gave Sally the attention that she deserved but instead he gave all the attention to his son. Ironically at the end of his life, his son couldn't be bothered to visit his dying father. His daughter Sally, who again was not shown much attention or love, was the one who stepped in and took care of him. When it came down to the reading of the will, the son was completely shocked to find out that he did not inherit a single dollar of the estate.

I asked Sally "would you change anything, if you could, with the lack of attention you received from your father during childhood, considering who you became because of the experience?"

Sally's reply was: "No, I wouldn't change a thing because he taught me in an indirect way how important it was to pay attention to your kids. I learned through this adversity (his lack of attention towards me) that I would not treat my kids the way he treated me and because of that, I have outstanding relationships with my children and my grandchildren."

With adversity you can choose to either let it bring you to a negative place and wallow in the misery using it as an excuse as to why you are not happy with yourself, or you can propel yourself to a higher place by learning from the obstacle and becoming a better and more forgiving person. Everyone deals with some type of adversity in this world; use yours to your advantage. Learn from the adversity so that others can benefit from your experience. *It is not the experience that changes a person; it is what they do with that knowledge from the experience that changes a person for better or worse.* Always take the high road and improve yourself from what you have experienced so that others can benefit from your knowledge.

There is a great story I read a few years in a book called *Streams in the Desert* which talks about a man who was watching a butterfly come out of its cocoon. He witnessed the butterfly struggling to get out of the small opening in the cocoon. Thinking that he could help the butterfly get out quicker, he took a pair of scissors and cut a wider opening in the cocoon to help the butterfly get out. Consequently, the butterfly was able to get out of the cocoon through the wider opening but unfortunately his wings did not work. The man quickly realized that Mother Nature has intentionally made it difficult for the butterfly to get out of the opening because when the butterfly squeezes through the natural small opening it helps to develop the wings. By having the man-made opening the butterfly never had a chance to fully develop its wings because it never applied the pressure that it needed by squeezing through the naturally small opening.

Life is not meant to be easy. Anthony Robbins, a well-known motivational speaker, is famous for talking about building "emotional muscle". Just like repetition will build up muscle mass in your body, hardships will build up emotional muscle in your mind. Life challenges and hardships will have the same effect, if you take a positive outlook on the experience.

> *"What doesn't kill you makes you stronger."*
> — Nietzsche

> *"Sometimes you have to live in darkness in order to appreciate the light."*
> — unknown

EMPLOYEES:

The next time you are about to feel sorry for yourself because you lost a deal or because you missed a promotion, stop and evaluate what went wrong. Try to strengthen yourself and your skills by understanding what you now need to do to succeed when faced with a similar situation in the future. If you look at any successful business person today they will usually say "I went through the school of hard knocks" or "it was sink or swim" or "I was just thrown in with the wolves." What they are doing is mentioning that it was not easy for them either, that they did not have all the answers and they too made mistakes. The lesson to learn here is to learn from your adversity and/or mistakes. Experience is often referred to as a guide, but is will only be useful if you can identify through your mistakes what behavior has to be changed, accepted or repeated. Consider your difficult experiences as the basic building blocks of your foundation. Without it, you would be weak and unable to deal with pressure, effectively.

MANAGERS:

Years ago, when I worked for an eye surgeon, I recall hearing worthy advice that stated "Surgeons aren't paid their high salaries to perform routine operations; they are paid their high salaries to know what to do when complications occur during routine surgery with patients."

What does this mean to a manager? When things are going great because you have a fantastic staff and the economy is doing well, it is very easy to rest on your laurels or past accomplishments. But when things are not going well, this is the crucial time to learn from your mistakes and grow from them. It is when business is not going so smoothly that you are going to learn what is of value to your clients. If a client leaves and transfers their business to a competitor, it is crucial to find out why and to eradicate the problem.

For example, if the client left because of a billing issue, then once you have a chance to identify the exact problem and to remedy it, the learning begins. The entire company that you work for should learn from a mistake like this to identify new procedures in billing to reinforce with the entire staff to insure it never happens again. In the long run this adversity improved the corporate billing policy and improved training procedures with each employee.

Everyone should be trained to look forward to making mistakes not because they want to look weak but because if they handle it in the right manner everyone will benefit from the experience and the company will grow. The manager should be the leader in this. From time to time, when the manager makes a mistake, they should openly confess to making the mistake and demonstrate how the company benefits from the mistake by showing the employees what not to do in a similar situation. This will give employees an example to follow and to realize that it is okay to admit a mistake. We should be ready to take on problems when they occur and have the attitude to want to share our experience when we do make a mistake to the staff so that everyone can learn from the situation and be better prepared the next time when a similar situation arises. Making mistakes is always going to be part of life and part of business. Coach your staff to take the high road, don't use a mistake as a crutch, use it to make yourself stronger and influence others to do the same to make the company stronger.

"Difficulties strengthen the mind as labor does the body."
— Seneca

"Don't be afraid of opposition; remember a kite rises against not with the wind."
— Hamilton Wright Mabil

"Adversity, look forward to the obstacles because once you overcome them you will be that much wiser and stronger than you would have been without them."
— unknown

Life Lesson #6

Why you shouldn't criticize people.

I LEARNED THIS LESSON ON A personal level when I was 11 years old. My brother, sisters and I were at our grandmother's house in Lynwood, New Jersey in the summer of 1982. We had just spent the day playing outside. All of the kids had come into the house and were lounging around in the living room. The conversation between the kids started to focus on my mother. First it was about how she always made us kids clean up the bathroom and our bedrooms. Then it started to get more personal. My aunt, who was 12 years old, brother and sisters started to criticize all the little things that she did to annoy them. I remember having a queasy feeling in my stomach while this verbal attack was taking place. I remained silent and listened but did not encourage them to shut up.

The conversation lasted for about 15 minutes with my aunt, brother and sisters stating criticism after criticism about my mother, such as how she dressed with her polyester pants, how she talked with her Scottish accent, how she embarrassed us when she picked us up in her old wooden paneled station wagon, etc. Just then there was a creak on the floor in the kitchen and there was my mom crying with tears streaming down her cheeks. She had heard the entire conversation. This was one of the worst moments of my life when I realized that my mom had heard her sister-in-law and children criticize who she was. No one could ever take any of that hurt away. No apology in the world would make her forget what she heard that day.

That experience reinforced in me that I would never again bring down a person like that or allow it to happen to anyone in front of me. It does not pay to criticize. Just like in kindergarten, it is always wise to follow the rule "if you don't have anything nice to say don't say anything at all" and better yet, walk out of the room or even ask the people engaged in the criticizing to stop.

"If a person is not there to defend themselves, don't criticize them."
— unknown

"Be nice to the people on your way up because you'll always meet them on your way down." — Jimmy Durante

Lesson 28

Be grateful for what you have.

TAKE A MOMENT AND BE GRATEFUL for everything that you have in your life today. Be grateful for your health, community, friends, children, education, talents, etc. Is there anything else you can be grateful for? For your wife, your husband, your ability to walk, talk, see and hear? Through some thoughtful advice from my boss, Mark Christo, I lie down next to my husband and children once a week and ask them individually what they are grateful for in their life today. My children usually state things like "I am grateful for Mommy and Daddy, for my brother or sister, and for my health. I am also grateful for my bike, for the ice cream we had today and for going swimming at the pool, etc." For you parents out there, I highly recommend trying this exercise at home with your kids because it is such a great non-intrusive way to find out what your children are thinking about and appreciating. The answers you receive from your spouse or significant other are great reinforcements for your relationship and for your own awareness. This precious time of reflection will help to remind you and your family what is really important.

According to recent studies, 60% of all health problems are stress related. This is reason enough not to let the little things in life affect your health. Prioritize your feelings of overwhelm when life gets to be too much, take a deep breath and think of what you are grateful for with the things that you have and the people in your life. Then realize that everything else is secondary.

A great way to reduce your stress level is to volunteer your time with someone less fortunate. I personally have a very ill mother who was diagnosed with Alzheimer's at 48 years of age. My mother, Mary Ellen Connolly, has been battling the disease for 12 years now. She is currently in a convalescent home and has been for over 9 years now. My mother is in her last stage of Alzheimer's where she can't walk, talk, feed herself or even eat (she is fed intravenously). I usually visit her on a Sunday with my kids and it is one of the most convincing moments each week for me to be grateful for what I can do physically and mentally. I am reminded of how grateful I am to be able to walk or run, talk to people and taste great food. I am also grateful to be able to write this book, to play with my kids and to make decisions about my life and my health. All of this is free and most people can do all of these common occurrences on a daily basis as well. Be grateful for all that you can do, experience life to its fullest. Don't just sit on the couch watching TV, get out there and enjoy the free things in life. One day, these common abilities and activities you've taken for granted might not be so easily accomplished.

Remember to focus on what is real and what you already have, not what you don't have. Be grateful for your health, listen to great music, enjoy beautiful flowers, taste great food, enjoy time spent with family and friends, help others in the community, etc.

> *"If you are of value to your friends, family and community,*
> *then you truly are a success."* — Einstein

EMPLOYEES:

Be grateful for the job that you currently have because there are so many people today that would do anything to be employed. There are so many reasons why people enjoy their jobs. Here are a few of the more popular reasons why people like their jobs:

I like my job because:

"I like to help people."
"I like the people that I work with."
"It is a short commute from home."
"I am constantly learning something new."
"The hours are great for my family."
"The benefits are great."
"They are closed on all holidays and I get 2 weeks paid vacation."
"Traveling all over the world is exciting."
"It is so exciting to work with such well known products and to have such customer loyalty with the brands."
"The money is great."

The list is endless as to what people can love about a job. Interestingly, these are reasons why people will also stay in a job even when they do not like the tasks that they are assigned to do, because the benefits outweigh the detriments. Many times, these same people have already experienced a long commute or an environment where people were not friendly. They might have been in an environment where there was no learning going on or because the pay was always being reduced due to poor budgetary reasons. These same people are so grateful of their working conditions that they have made a choice based on knowing that it is not greener on the other side or that the benefit of working with positive, fun people outweighs finding another career. Just something to think about. . . . Take the time to identify the positive qualities about your current job.

Be grateful for those qualities. At the same time, compare those positive qualities to the negative qualities. Then write down what you absolutely enjoy about your job. For example: If you are in sales and you love dealing with people but you are tired of "pounding the phone for appointments," look into a trainer position or an account manager position where you can manage an account for a company and still do what you do best which is deal with people.

Having excellent interpersonal skills is an asset. Those skills are also used in management. Don't limit yourself to always having to do sales if you are tired of the making sales calls. Look at alternative ways to work internally with people in a company but still use what you are good at.

MANAGERS:

From a retention standpoint, managers should always be aware of what current benefits the company offers for the medical, dental and financial plans, as well as the insurance programs and/or gym memberships, etc. It is highly advised to review the actual plans periodically to keep abreast of what the company is paying out on premiums and what the employees have to contribute to, in reference to their prescription co-pays, their doctor visit co-pays and of course the deductibles that have to be met before the coverage kicks in with emergency hospital visits. Managers need to stay informed of these inevitable changes in the insurance industry and listen to the complaints from employees. *Many of these complaints are telltale signs that employees might leave for better coverage if something is not done to change the policy.* Companies need to stay competitive with their competition's policies. This is especially relevant to small companies that do not have a dedicated human resource representative that manages the benefits. These managers will need to go the extra mile and inquire about the current benefit plan policies to ensure that their employees won't leave because the policy was not competitive or updated. Their due diligence should pay off for everyone involved not just for retaining the good employees but for reducing the costs that managers pay into for their own insurance premiums and co-pays.

It is also the manager's job to remind the employees to participate in the benefit programs. Partipation can increase an employee's health and well-being, morale, stability and financial security. Companies also benefit when their employees participate in the company-sponsored benefit programs because they in return usually receive employees who are happier because they are medically insured and more financially secure, which means they will probably be retained longer.

For example, the financial investment programs (401k, stock option, etc.) help to retain the talented employees because they will usually be able to receive some type of matching from the company, and allows their nest egg to grow larger than it would if they weren't in that specific company-sponsored program. Many companies will also require that an employee be vested for a specific amount of years in order to be able to touch the funds. This is often referred to as the golden handcuffs. It is a win-win situation for everyone because the employee stays with a company for a specific period of time (usually longer than they would have without the plan) and in return the company usually matches or donates on a quarterly basis a percentage to the employee's investment account.

If there is a tuition reimbursement program, encourage all employees to take courses that are related to their field. If the company has a softball or bowling league, encourage them to join the team. By encouraging your employees to participate in these company-sponsored programs, your employees will start to build an appreciation for the company, a bond that is not just about work but about appreciating what the company does for them outside of the job.

If your company provides any type of benefit, be grateful for those benefits. If your company does not, inquire as to when they might be implemented. Take the time to research the costs of a new benefit. If you believe the company can afford that benefit for everyone, bring it up in a meeting. If the company rejects the benefit due to budget constraints, look into affording the benefit yourself. For example: if your company does not have a 401K program, set one up yourself. You do not need a company-sponsored program to set up an investment account. Speak to a local financial advisor for more information.

Lesson 29

"Happiness is an inside job."
— William Arthur Ward

I FIRST HEARD THIS QUOTE from Jim Rohn, one of the most influential motivational speakers in the circuit today. What a true statement, "happiness" really does come from within ourselves. This coincides with the previous grateful statement. It is important to accept that you can't rely on anything to have to happen in the future to make you happy today; happiness can be inside you right this moment. Many people will set an internal standard or goal stating when they have a better job they will be happy, or when they get a raise or promotion they will be happy or when they have a new baby they will be happy. Life does not work that way! Your current state of mind can and will make you happy. If you want to be happy, then be happy. If you need a few examples as to why you should be happy versus sad, then here it goes:

Example #1

Be happy because no one likes a miserable person except for another miserable person!

Example #2

Be happy because being happy is contagious. Smile at the next person that you meet and see if they smile back. When they do, it will make you feel good, all because you felt happy. ☺

Example #3

Most companies durng the interview process will reject a competent applicant who complained a lot during the interview process. They will instead hire a more junior applicant with a positive attitude all because no one likes to work with a person who is negative.

As mentioned earlier in January of 1999, I attended a 5-day seminar about values. The seminar was an enlightening experience to say the least. Many of the exercises that were presented dealt with understanding your own values and why they were important to you personally. One particular exercise had a tremendous impact on me, and because of the outcome, I want to share it with all of you so you can benefit also. This exercise is intended to bring a person to a positive frame of mind in seconds.

(Please note that this exercise will take only a few minutes.) Think back in time to an event in your life when you were happy. Maybe it was a major achievement of yours with a major sense of accomplishment such as the moment you graduated from high school, college or graduate school. Maybe it was the moment you had your first child or the moment you received an award or closed a big deal? Bring yourself back to that moment. You probably have a smile or a grin on your face right now (if you brought yourself back to that moment). Have you found a memorable moment yet? Take the time to put this book down and think hard. There has to be at least one moment in your life that you are proud of. Got one? Good. Think about where you were, who was with you? Your heart was probably racing, maybe you were smiling from ear to ear or maybe internally you felt as if you were unstoppable, or on top of the world? It feels great doesn't it? Take the time to revisit this event one more time. Doesn't it feel good to remember a time when you were so proud of yourself? *Capture that memory.* Do you like the way that memory has made you feel temporarily? Do you feel more confident, like you can take on the world? Do you feel like you felt when you experienced that event for the first time? Is there any reason why you shouldn't feel that way all the time? Please realize that this "sense of accomplishment" is free, inside your mind at all times. Free to retrieve and refer to at a moment's notice. You have many of those accomplishments or moments that should keep you feeling positive all the time. Use this exercise often and it will constantly remind you that you are capable of achieving anything you set your mind to and that it is up to you to be happy or sad, no one else.

From a business perspective practice this exercise before a big interview, important meeting or just when you need a little extra confidence in yourself. You have already proven to yourself that you can accomplish great deeds. If this is what you need to get back into the swing of things to stay positive and keep pursuing your goals, then keep reinforcing the positive memories whenever you need a good positive boost! It's free inside your mind all the time.

Jim Rohn is famous for saying:

"A successful year begins with successful days; that means successful tasks each day. Manage your time with positive efforts toward your goals every day."

Your well disciplined efforts of planning correctly will still be limited if you are going through the motions with a negative attitude. A negative attitude will push business away instead of attract business. If your job is to attract business and to get people to believe in you, then get into the habit of doing this exercise before every business call or meeting. No one else can give you happiness but yourself and that happiness is already inside of you waiting to come out. Don't rely on any future event to be happy, be happy now! Please remember happiness truly is an inside job!

EMPLOYEES:

Start your day each day by knowing that you are in charge of your state of mind. If there are employees in the office that constantly complain, avoid them. A negative state of mind is very contagious, so try to avoid the people who are negative if possible. If this is impossible, then at least don't agree with them when they do complain. Listen to them vent but don't agree or disagree. This will also keep a person out of trouble by never agreeing or disagreeing to gossip or complaints about work-related issues. Set up a goal in the morning to accomplish a certain task. Maybe it is to organize your desk? Then accomplish the task. There will be a major sense of accomplishment that a person will feel when the task is accomplished, no matter how big or small the task was. FYI: A person's desk can reflect what is taking place mentally. If an employee's desk has papers scattered all over the table-top on a regular basis, then it usually is an indication that the employee is not in control of their daily job responsibilities; that they are overwhelmed with their current job responsibilities and that many critical steps are probably being overlooked or not followed on a daily basis. Take the time to learn to take control of your daily activities. By organizing your desk, you will start to organize your thoughts which will allow you to prioritize your days instead of waiting for the priority work to become a "fire" to put out.

The next time you go into work, look at the desks of the highly productive employees. Their desks are probably neat, right? There is a reason why they are productive and it is because they have taken the time to organize their thoughts by eliminating anything that would be a distraction. This activity will also help them to never feel overwhelmed. This is yet another way to help to feel in control and happy on the job. Make sure throughout the day that you set up tasks and complete those tasks because when you do, you will give yourself a small, positive sense of accomplishment. Even a small task such as organizing a desk, once you do it, will help you to feel good about yourself and will be a good reminder that you are a capable person who can accomplish anything you set your mind to. Big or small.

"Work smarter not harder."
— Jim Rohn

"We are all given the same amount of time during the day, it is what we consider a priority that we do that separates us."
— Jim Rohn

MANAGERS:

Be a good leader. Obviously, there will be times when situations in the office will cause everyone to not want to be too "happy". This is an acceptable part of business. Because of this, it is your responsibility to make sure you are a leader who your employees will want to follow especially during the tough times. Stay positive and happy on the job. Reinforce with your employees the importance of being up and positive.

For example: If an employee is in a bad mood even during one transaction with a customer and does not give their all, the consequences can be devastating for the business if they handle the wrong customer at the wrong time.

Train your employees to expect difficult situations to arise because it is all part of running a business. Encourage your staff to look forward to these situations with an open mind, to learn from it and hopefully increase service because of the experience. It is also wise to reinforce with your staff to always stand by their values. If the competition is doing something that is immoral and/or illegal yet getting the business currently that your company wants, encourage with your employee that a person with high values will in the long run succeed and a person with low values will eventually get what they deserve. Treat other people the way you want to be treated. Don't have your employees lower their standards by doing something that is illegal just because the competition is doing it. When a situation like this happens, praise your staff members for having such high values. Reinforce in them that they should never lower their standards to get the business. They should instead always rise above the situation. At this point the employees with high values should be grateful they are not working for a company that has to resort to such low-class business practices or illegal practices to gain business. In summation, happiness truly is an inside job. Always stay in a positive frame of mind. Use this exercise when you need an extra boost. Be happy and reinforce with your employees to be happy, too!

Lesson 30

Help other people to help yourself.

EVERYONE IN THE WORLD should attend and participate in charity events or get involved in fundraising events. The experience of working for one of these events is so uplifting and personally rewarding. Besides the obvious benefit that charities do for those in need, it also benefits the workers who get involved by allowing them to step away from their own problems and by helping others who are less fortunate. The experience helps to reinforce in a person what is truly important in the world. No longer is money or possessions a constant focus. Instead one will realize that health, happiness, being able to see, hear and the ability to get around physically without pain is often taken for granted. The financial or personal problems that a person had going into an event often get reduced in size due to a reality check when a person gets a chance to meet a family that has just gone through the tragedy of losing a child or parent to cancer, etc.

Make it a habit to get out in the community, get to know your neighbors, donate blood, support the local fire department, donate food to the local food bank, give a free seminar on a topic that you know well enough to help others in need, volunteer your time to help others in the community by doing chores for them, volunteer at your local hospital, spend a few hours picking up trash in your neighborhood, plant flowers in your neighborhood, donate your time at a charity walk, etc. The list is endless and the rewards are priceless.

> *"If you are of value to your friends, family and community, then you truly are a success."*
> — Einstein

> *"I'm too busy, I have no time for worry."*
> — Winston Churchill

EMPLOYEES:

To get involved in local charity events, ask your human resources department about local events. Want to do something yourself? Call the local Red Cross office and ask to set up a blood drive or organize a drive for Toys for Tots by encouraging employees to bring in unwrapped presents for needy families during the holidays. Not only will the experience be rewarding in itself but you will also benefit by getting to know other employees outside of work and get a chance to network with business people from the community.

MANAGERS:

Be an excellent leader for your employees by supporting charity events. Motivate your entire staff to participate in a local charity event; the experience will help to facilitate team building between your own employees and introduce others to a lifelong commitment of supporting charities and helping others that are less fortunate. There is also an added value to having employees from the same company participate in charity events and that is that people take notice by remembering which companies and employees took the time to participate. By participating in charity events, a company's image of being a company that cares and one that encourages their own employees to take the time to support charities is projected in the community. This action could be the swing vote for someone that is considering doing business with a specific company or choosing to work for that company. The biggest payoff from participating in charity events is the ability to help others. It is a priceless reward to get a chance to give back to the community by helping someone else who is less fortunate in addition to getting a chance to put the small personal problems into perspective. Get involved today with a local charity today, the rewards are endless!

Life Lesson #7

Do one act of kindness a day.

WHILE GROWING UP IN GERMANY for 7 years because my father was in the army, I learned to appreciate beautiful, clean cobblestone streets. In Germany, very rarely do you see discarded beer cans, coffee cups or fast food containers on the ground. The reason why the citizens of Germany do not have litter on the ground is because everyone takes pride, every day, to maintain their part of the sidewalk or road. Germany strictly enforces anti-litter laws. If a person is caught littering, they are fined the equivalent of $400 to $500 dollars or more. I was so appalled when my family moved back to the States as a teenager to see cigarette butts, coffee cups, soda and beer cans, sneakers and fast food containers littered on the ground. It still baffles me to this day how a person can have the audacity to throw an empty soda can on the ground, not for the sake of getting fined (in areas where the litter laws are in effect which aren't many) but just for conducting the actual act of thinking that it is okay to litter.

One night after dinner in October of 2002, I took a walk with my daughter Gracie, who was 5 years old at the time. We walked around our neighborhood for about half an hour talking about the day's events. While on the walk Gracie saw a piece of litter on the ground and said while pointing to the litter, "Mommy, look. Someone just littered. I will pick it up and put it in the trash can". So she skipped to the nearest trashcan in the neighborhood and opened the lid and put it in. (It was garbage night so everyone's trash can was already on the side of the road.) I was very impressed with Gracie's actions and let her know that she did a good deed.

A few moments later she spotted a second piece of trash and said "Mommy, oh no, another person littered!" I said to her, "Gracie, you are such a good person for picking up the litter, if only every person in the world picked up just one piece of litter a day, the world would be a much cleaner place." Gracie turned to me and said, "Mommy, I think I should pick up a few more pieces because not everyone picks up their litter." Isn't that so true?

Did you know that performing an act of kindness stimulates the same area of the brain as physical pleasure? Both cause the release of endorphins. This release of endorphins should be just one of many reasons why people should want to help other people or perform one act of kindness per day, selfishly because it makes them feel good. Can you think of a person who doesn't want to feel good? Anyone? Make a point everyday to help someone by picking up one piece of trash, donating something to charity, complimenting a hardworking waitperson or acknowledging the hard work of an employee or co-worker or personally by letting your spouse know that they are appreciated. All of these acts of kindness cost nothing monetarily but the return on investment is tenfold. Establish a daily habit of doing something nice for someone; you will become a role model for someone else by influencing them to do the same. A great movie to watch that supports a similar concept is "Pay It Forward". Rent it when you can.

On September 11, 2002, I attended a seminar in New York City with the "NYC Powerteam", lead by Dr. Robert Carrow. This is a networking group that is comprised of employees and volunteers who have worked with Anthony Robbins over the years. This group of 30-40 people keep their motivation up by conducting their own coaching and motivational exercises by bringing in speakers on all types of topics involving self-development, career enhancement, financial security and charity events. That evening we had three speakers talk about their past year's events since the World Trade Center tragedy, where over 3000 innocent people died in New York City, due to terrorist activity. Each of the speakers were directly affected by losing a fiancé, wife or husband. The speakers talked about what had changed about themselves since the tragedy. The common theme amongst all three speakers was they had increased the amount of kindness that they gave on a daily basis. One went as far as to create a website about kindness. When people go through devastating loss, they always seem to be more understanding to other people. What I took away from that night was why wait until you experience such loss to start doing one act of kindness a day? The endorphin release alone should be enough of a reason to make yourself feel better by helping someone else, right?

EMPLOYEES:

As an employee, you should be proud of the place where you work. If you are walking into your office building and see an empty container on the ground or a piece of discarded paper, pick it up. If you see something on the carpet that should be in the garbage, pick it up. Perform one act of kindness a day because it will make you feel good and might possibly influence someone else to do one act of kindness, too! The next time you are in a store and receive excellent service, take the time to tell the person that is waiting on you that they were very fast or very courteous. It will make their day and yours, too. One act of kindness, pass it on!

MANAGERS:

Lead by example. If you see trash on the floor or outside the entrance of the office building, clean it up. If you take the staff out for lunch and the food is delicious, make sure you tell the manager or tell the waiter to give "compliments to the chef" for an excellent meal. This will make you feel good to give the compliment, reinforce to the chef that they are excellent at what they do and show your employees the importance of complimenting excellent service. In addition, every once in a while, buy your employees lunch or give them free tickets to a show, play, ballgame, etc. Show them that you appreciate their loyalty and dedication. At the very least, send them an email that states that they did a good job or let them know how much you appreciate all of their hard work in front of their colleagues. One of the classic complaints I hear from my clients who are thinking of leaving their current job is that their boss never showed any appreciation for all of their hard work. Show appreciation. Employees certainly appreciate when their manager says "job well done!" In truth they need it. Always remember that as a role model you are teaching tomorrow's managers how to appreciate people. Go the extra mile every day to teach your employees the trait of doing one act of kindness every day. This habit will clearly benefit generations of people as great leaders in many aspects of life no matter what the action is, complimenting people or cleaning up after others.

Lesson 31

*Show respect to the people
who have the authority to fire you.*

I LEARNED A VALUABLE LESSON during a managers meeting in the fall of 2002 that evolved into the following chapter of remembering to show respect to the people who have the authority to fire you.

It was customary with every manager meeting that the facilitator of the meeting, a.k.a. my boss, would always start the meeting by stating "we can agree to disagree" so that the "meeting of the minds" could come up with solutions to problems by challenging an idea from a colleague. These meetings always produced creative ideas and solutions.

This current meeting had been called due to my request to implement a formal "interview sheet" for all new candidates that were interviewed in all of the offices. It had been apparent to me for several years that the interview process was different in every office which was causing employee files in the database to lack consistency and critical data that was needed to make a sound decision for assigning an employee to a job or project. At that time, I had just opened an office in Norwalk, CT. The office was already billing out $3 million a year. In total, I was one of the only offices that was trying to streamline the processes and procedures in order to gain some consistency in the database so that more informed decisions could be made about qualified candidates that had already been interviewed.

For an entire year from 2001-2002 prior to the meeting, I had made improvements on a monthly basis on the interview sheet with my staff by tweaking changes with additions and removal of questions that we all observed to be working or not working in order to increase the sheet's effectiveness. Once the sheet was introduced, it immediately started to increase the information gathered from the interview into the database which helped to standardize the interview process so that everyone was receiving consistent information. Finally the right information was being entered into the database such as:

- Why the person left their last job?
- What were their motivating reasons for leaving their last/current job?
- What type of projects have they worked on?
- What was their last year's salary?
- What were their strengths/weaknesses?

The new sheet also improved each recruiter's performance by teaching them to give a better interview, which helped to increase word of mouth referrals. In addition to giving a better interview, the interview sheet helped to decrease the amount of time it took to identify a candidate in the database based on the information from the interview. Throughout the year, I had excitedly shared my new interview sheet with my boss to let him know that the other offices could benefit from it as well. Throughout my entire career with the Monroe Group, I have always enjoyed improving processes and sharing new ideas, especially ones that are accepted. This is certainly one of the rewards of working for a small business that is rapidly expanding.

The meeting could not come soon enough in the last quarter of 2002. I was so excited for the meeting due to the positive impact a company-approved interview sheet would make on increasing productivity, continuity and consistency for the entire company. By that time I was aware that my boss was reviewing other interview sheets submitted by other offices. Realistically, I did not expect my boss to implement my new sheet entirely but I certainly expected some portions of the interview sheet to be accepted. To my surprise, he got up and spoke about the need for streamlining the process of the interview sheet and implemented to all of the offices a completely different interview sheet, one that was very generic, antiquated and did not meet the needs of all of the offices.

Needless to say, I was shocked and disappointed. He did not even implement a portion of the interview sheet that I had already proven to be successful. *Please pay close attention as I share with you a situation you may encounter with your superiors in the near future.*

Once my boss had announced the selected interview sheet, I raised my hand during the meeting and said "I thoroughly understand and agree that all of the offices need to agree to use the same interview sheet in order to improve our continuity and consistency in the database. In fact, I have been aware of this issue for a while and because of that I created and improved our interview sheet in Norwalk a year ago. For the past year my office has used, utilized, tweaked and improved the sheet on a monthly basis to where it is today. And because of all of our efforts our interview sheet is more advanced than what is being implemented today. We also had a proven track record of success by consistently using the standard interview questions. As you may recall over the past year I have shared that with you several times. My question is, are you asking my office to also use this interview sheet that is being presented today or can my office use the sheet that we have adopted for the past year?"

His answer to me was "Lisa, you must use the process I am implementing and my word is final." Well, from previous experience, our meetings had always been a great "meetings of the minds" and every discussion had generated new and creative ideas for implementation. At that moment I was furious and my face showed it, I had temporarily lost my cool and it was showing in my facial expressions and the redness in my face and neck. I personally thought about walking out the door and quitting at that exact moment. I knew my interview sheet was a major improvement to what he was implementing and because of that I decided not to *react but to respond*, calmly.

Through experience, I also knew my boss well enough to know that he had made an unintentional oversight. Out of respect for him, being the owner of a $24 million dollar company at the time and also being my boss, I responded to his statement by requesting that I would like to speak to him personally about this new interview sheet after the meeting. He agreed.

After the meeting, we talked and he agreed that the interview sheet that he had implemented during the meeting was not a match for my office and that he would allow my office to use the more advanced sheet. I was satisfied with his response and was thrilled that I could still use the interview sheet that had a great track record of success in my office. What came next was a major surprise! Later that day I received an email from him that stated:

> "Lisa, I certainly respect your opinion and everything that you do for this company every day, but one of the things that I never do is approach people in front of others. If there is a problem or a discrepancy, please don't try to tear down and attack. You may have disagreed with what I want you to do, but you could have handled it in a much better way. I felt that as the conversation went on you compromised my authority and certainly challenged it."

Well, to say the least, I was extremely disturbed by the email. Not only did I think that I handled the situation in a professional manner, but I had also talked to him after the meeting and resolved the situation. *The problem was we were fighting about two different subjects!* He was upset with me because

I had not shown him the respect that he wanted when I apparently challenged his authority. I was upset because he did not show me the respect that I deserved for working on the new interview sheet for a year, in addition to the fact that I was the one that requested to implement a companywide interview sheet in the first place!

The previous chapter on understanding the situation from both sides is also very important in this situation. *The big factor in this situation was that he had the authority to fire me at any moment and it was up to me to either swallow my pride and keep my job or stand up for what I felt was right.* Although I considered quitting at that moment for the reason that I knew I was in the right with the new sheet, the truth was I did not feel like searching for a new job and I really liked my job and the company. *The lessons that I learned from this experience are to show respect to the people who have authority to fire you, especially when you are in a meeting with other co-workers by not challenging them, and to never make a decision when you are emotionally charged or upset.*

EMPLOYEES:

As an employee, always show respect to the people that are high in the ranks of the company. If you do disagree with them, talk to them one on one. Don't compromise their authority in front of anyone, even if the policy is a "meeting of the minds."

Once again, when debates get heated, don't make a decision when you are emotionally charged or upset. Take the emotion out of it, cool off by getting a glass of water or take a few deep breaths to rationalize your reaction. Don't react but instead respond intelligently. Try to see the viewpoint of the other person. Remember that *they* are probably not as emotionally attached to the decision as you are.

MANAGERS:

As a manager or an owner, if you are going to roll out a new process that will affect the entire company, especially when the process is to streamline the procedures or implement new guidelines. It is highly suggested that a process improvement committee be created that would include a member of each department that would be affected by the change. This will make sure that the "new process" benefits all that are directly affected by the change. If changes or exceptions have to be made then address it before the "new process" is implemented so that no one will feel neglected or adversely affected.

Additionally, this is also a valuable lesson to reinforce the power of learning from experience. I was definitely at fault for confronting my boss in front of the management staff; it is important to always know your limitations as an employee. I have learned never to do this again, but it does not stop there as a manager. I shared this experience with my staff to show them that no one is perfect. I wanted them to understand the valuable lesson of "showing respect to people in the ranks" so that I might prevent them from making the same mistake that I did.

I am also an advocate of requesting that people remove the emotion from business. When an employee or manager does not agree with a change or decision, they must think about their response. If they are upset by a change, they must evaluate why they are upset. Next, they should take the emotion out of it and try to see it from a business standpoint. By putting themselves in their boss's shoes, they should be able to see the viewpoint and the rationalization of why the change was implemented without jeopardizing their job.

- "Act, don't react."
- "Reaction rearranged equals Creation" — Dr. Robert Carrow
- "Don't react but respond!"

Lesson 32

"If you are confused, be excited,
it means you are about to learn something."
— Anthony Robbins

THE PREVIOUS CHAPTER talked about showing respect for your superiors by not attacking them in front of other superiors or colleagues and to instead approach them on a one on one basis when you need to resolve a disagreement. It was also a good reminder to respond, not react to situations. Thankfully there was yet another lesson that I gained from this specific experience. It occurred a few days after the meeting and the infamous "e-mail" from my boss, Mark. For days I had been confused from the events that had occurred since the meeting. Over the years I had always shown a great deal of respect to Mark in front of the staff. What I didn't understand was how he had interpreted my feedback as an "attack". As mentioned earlier, when the company was in its infancy stage we had always given constructive feedback to each other and he always stressed in meetings that it was okay to disagree, often times saying "we agree to disagree."

I was confused because I did not like the position that I had been accused "of verbally attacking" my boss in a meeting. For the past five years I had devoted my career to the company, working countless hours of overtime, working through lunch almost every day, working on the weekends to get projects done, etc. Does this sound familiar? Have you been in a situation similar to this? Have you ever thought of quitting because you were so mad? Well, don't quit just yet! To my surprise, an additional lesson came out of this learning experience. A bonus lesson that could prevent others from making the mistake of leaving a great company is about to be shared, please read on.

As I had mentioned before, three days had gone by since the infamous e-mail. I had restless nights sleep, wasn't focusing 100% on my business and last but not least was confused about my career. I enjoyed my salary and I truly valued my clients. I knew one thing and that was that I did not want to look for a new job in my current state of mind.

On the fourth day after the email, I had an awakening. Over the years I had often seen Anthony Robbins (author of *Awaken The Giant Within*) get excited in public seminars whenever someone would raise their hand to ask Anthony advice on a problem. The person from the audience would often start the question off by saying "Anthony, I am confused". At that point he would always make a point of getting everyone in the audience excited that the person said they were "confused" because to him it meant that the person was about to learn something new *if* they stated what they were confused about. After the person in the audience stated why they were confused, Anthony would then apply some of his well researched techniques to rewire their thinking or their interpretation of a past event or experience that was confusing them. He would say something like "being temporarily confused means that you are about to grow. This is because you are about to learn something that you did not know before."

That was it! I was confused about the past days events and I was about to grow because I discovered what the answer was to my question. I realized that my old style of contributing ideas to new processes when the company was very small (infancy state) with only 2 offices had worked well. My problem was that the company had grown at that point to 7 offices and I was still using my 2 office mentality. No wonder I was confused! What I had learned was that my boss had adapted a new style of management that he started practicing probably a few months or even a year prior to keep up with the growth of the company. He had to change his style of management because he had grown from 15 employees to 40, from a $17 million dollar company to a $23 million dollar company all in 4 years. The company changed so he changed. It grew so he grew in order to keep up with the demands and the pace. *I finally realized that I had not changed my management style and that was why I was confused! The only way I was going to keep my job and stay happy on the job was to change my management style and match it to the needs of the company.*

A feeling of exultation came upon me. I was no longer confused. I called Mark that morning and explained that I realized that I was at fault, not for implementing a new process, but for not changing my management style to adapt to the growth of the company. What worked in the past was not going to work in the future because the company had evolved. Needless to say, he was very happy to hear me say those words. An immediate sense of relief came off my shoulders and I was no longer confused. I had never been happier in the company.

How many times have you met a person and said to yourself "boy, have they changed!" Sometimes you see them in a negative light; sometimes it is a more positive one. What you have to realize is that they did what they had to do to survive in their job based on current conditions.

Management styles, new processes, rules, guidelines and new procedures are all established to help a business run more effectively. From a recruiting perspective, I see the benefit of a company hiring an employee that has just come from a well-processed environment to go to a company that is not so organized. That employee's experience from the well-processed environment will help them to improve processes and procedures by implementing new ideas learned from their prior company.

In short, if you have a creative idea, bring it up to your supervisor on a one on one basis. This will ensure that you have their attention 100% when you introduce the idea. Next, present the idea and tell them or show them why it would work by using specific examples as to why it is needed. If your idea is declined, respect the person by not making a scene publicly, but instead go back to the source and review why the idea is not accepted. Make sure you present all of the benefits and understand its full impact on the company, and don't forget about your presentation skills. Make it relative from their viewpoint and learning style.

"God grant me the serenity to accept the things I cannot change, the courage to change the things I can and the wisdom to know the difference."
— Serenity Prayer

EMPLOYEES:

If you are confused, be excited! It means you are about to grow! That does not mean to act stupid. No! It means give 100% of your attention to anything you do and when something just does not make sense to you, evaluate the situation. Have any variables changed? Is the company the same company that you started with? Do you report to more people now? Have your values changed? Have your company's values changed? Have you invested in yourself by constantly keeping up to date with the latest technology and advances in your career and industry? If you are confused, admit it, control your emotions and evaluate the situation to see if you can grow from the experience.

MANAGERS:

If and when you observe an employee acting confused or upset because of a business-related matter, bring them in, identify the situation and resolve it, if possible. Don't let the employee spin out of control. Once in the "spin cycle" that employee could affect employee morale, customer service, etc. Many times a confused employee will learn something new if given the right tools to understand the situation from both sides. Help your employees to constantly learn. As the company grows or decreases, share with them the monthly activities so they have a better business understanding. *It will help to keep everyone on the same team!*

Lesson 33

Managers and employees:
don't be best friends with co-workers.

THIS LESSON OF NOT BECOMING best friends with employees and managers is difficult to enforce, therefore employees and managers often have to learn this lesson the hard way by making the mistake first and learning the lesson second.

This rule of not being friends with co-workers is not saying don't be friendly, it is only saying prioritize your commitment to your career. Rationalize that the job you are hired for is probably by choice to earn a living. Make sure that you are always performing your job at your fullest ability by not allowing any emotions on the job to influence your best decision-making powers because of a conflict of interest with a friend that is also a co-worker or manager. This rule should be respected because there will be many times when a conflict of interest will arise between the friendship and the job. This conflict of interest will temporarily cause an employee to add emotion to a business decision that otherwise would have been an easy decision to make. When emotions from office friendships are involved, decisions can be swayed to benefit a friendship instead of making the best decision for the company.

Employee or co-worker favoritism can result in a temporary unbalanced working environment. To avoid this situation, employees and managers should always make a decision not to become emotionally involved with co-workers. The easiest way to prevent this is to not over-socialize with co-workers or managers outside of the work environment.

Understandably, there are many working environments where employees work long shifts and many days in a row, such as hospital and restaurant environments. Due to long shifts and lack of time off, it becomes very difficult for employees to network outside of work to meet and develop new friendships. It is in these environments especially where this rule has to be followed because conflicts of interest between managers and employees or between co-workers can develop. Why add more stress to an already stressful environment? Keep work and play separate.

Another situation that can arise is when a manager has to constructively criticize or even terminate an employee who is also their good friend. Not only does the business relationship suffer but so can the friendship. As mentioned before, close friendships in the office quite often negatively affect other employees. This can result in decreased office morale. It is critical to be aware that this rule is not telling you to not get personal with your employees. It is absolutely necessary to get to know and remember the names of your employee's spouse, children's names, sports teams that he/she follows, etc. What is being suggested is that employees and managers should try to avoid establishing a regular habit of going out on a regular basis. Those types of occasions should be isolated events to celebrate a victory, holiday, an accomplishment or to support a team-building event.

A follow-up suggestion when networking outside of work is for employees and managers to always stay in control of their alcohol intake if they choose to engage at all at any of the company-sponsored events. In addition, everyone needs to know their limitations at these events and follow them.

Fact: Managers and employees work for years to gain the respect they have earned in the office. It is frightful to think that just one night of excessive drinking with co-workers or superiors can diminish the hard-earned respect that took years to build.

In summation, network with employees to build the trust that is needed to do your job well but don't cross the line with developing strong friendships on the job with co-workers or managers. Instead, focus on the career first. Always keep work and play separate to avoid any uncomfortable situations that could compromise your decision-making judgment.

EMPLOYEES:

It is critical to not become best friends with your co-workers because *it can compromise your judgment with internal business decisions.* The following is an account of an actual conflict that occurred between two members of my staff who mistakenly became too close of friends on the job that caused added stress to an already stressful job.

Two employees, (names withheld) working in a small office of five staff members start to become very friendly with one another by going out for lunch together, shopping together at night after work, etc. One day they have a fight in the office over a personal issue which disrupts the entire office, slows business for a few hours and puts everyone in the office on edge. Immediately one of the employees asks for a transfer. The company does not approve the transfer request. Both employees are called into a meeting to resolve the situation in order to bring the office back to normality. Both employees are issued verbal warnings and are reminded that the next outburst can result in termination. Here is the ironic fact, this situation had nothing to do with on-the-job performance, yet it consequently could result in termination. Over the course of the next few weeks the verbal warnings have the two employees upset because they are now on probation. In addition they have anxiety towards each other in the office. At all costs, each employee is avoiding contact with the other. This avoidance/disconnect reduced office morale, communication and productivity. In the end, the situation resolved itself but it took months of "anxiety and duress" to learn the lesson that *co-workers* should stay co-workers and not engage in deep friendships on the job.

Hopefully this example shed some light as to why employees and managers should make friends elsewhere, not on the job. It is wise to keep your relationships on the job professional only. If this rule was enforced in every company on every level, it would eliminate so many unnecessary problems; yet many employees tend to ignore it and unfortunately their careers sometime suffer the consequences temporarily or permanently.

MANAGERS:

As a manager, enforce the rule of not being friends with your co-workers as much as possible. Make a point of reminding your employees to keep their relationships on a business level at all times. Remind your new hires about the risks of becoming too friendly with their co-workers. Give them examples as to why this rule is in place. Encourage them to use this lesson as a legitimate reason as to why they shouldn't mingle with employees outside of work when they are pressured to do so. Let them know it is a company policy. By enforcing this rule it will help to ensure that all workers are productive and focused when they are in the office and that all business decisions are not biased based on internal friendships or alliances. As a manager, remember not to break the rule either. Don't favor employees because they are your friends; it will only compromise your judgment and cause you to overlook other well-deserving employees for promotions or special projects. Office favoritism also creates an inhospitable working environment that is uncomfortable. Be a good leader by leading by example, keep friendships outside of work and make all business decisions using your best decision-making powers uninfluenced by favoritism towards others on the job.

Lesson 34

Manage all employees differently based on their level of competence.

CCORDING TO A RECENT STUDY conducted by the American Management Association, a huge percentage of employees leave companies not because of salary or benefits but due to poor management or lack of management. The unfortunate reality of this survey is that many managers are never given proper training to manage effectively in their current environment, which is causing this rapid exodus of dissatisfied employees.

With the speed of business today, often times high performing employees are promoted to management positions without prior management training. They are expected to immediately start performing as a manager before they ever receive any formal type of management training that relates to their industry. Unfortunately, when these newly promoted managers start to manage without any formal strategies, processes or guidelines to follow on how to guide, direct, delegate, manage, coach, hire, fire, constructively criticize, etc. . . . errors start to occur. In the medical industry, would you ever promote a nurse to a position of doctor without sending that person through medical school? Of course not! Well then, why do companies promote employees to positions of management without proper training? In a company environment, the results will be devastating if the management is incompetent.

So how do companies make sure that all managers are trained properly to manager others? Answer: The company first needs to make a commitment to every employee that they will provide excellent managers and leaders by investing in continuous management training before and after the manager receives the position to manage employees. Even if a current manager attended management training 5 years ago in a different industry, that same manager would still need to be sent to update, refresh and learn new skills that are relevant to their current company policies and expectations.

The next commitment the company needs to make is to the newly appointed manager. The company needs to set goals and expectations of the manager and then show that manager how they can accomplish the goals (as mentioned earlier). A company should never hire an employee and just state "hit this goal by March". The same rule applies with manager goal setting. The goal has to be stated and the steps necessary to accomplish the goal need to be provided. If the company does not provide the steps to the manager on how to accomplish the goal, then the company is supporting and training their manager incorrectly.

This lesson will not dictate which "type" of management style is the best type to follow, that all depends on the office environment and the industry that the manager is working in. What is being reinforced here is to mandate that every company should provide adequate management training for all of their newly promoted managers and to continuously provide on-going training for existing managers. When companies invest in their management on a regular basis they can expect their managers to receive some of the following benefits:

- The managers will become aware of alternative styles of management that just might be the solution they need to increase morale and productivity in specific situations. (One style of management when the company has only 20 employees might not be effective when the company grows to be 1,000 employees; managers must be ready and open to changing styles to be effective.)
- Through continuous management training, the manager will constantly be increasing their human relations skills, which to this day is still the most important criteria to being an effective manager.
- The managers will learn how to effectively delegate tasks to increase productivity while keeping employee moral high.
- Managers will learn how to effectively set expectations of their employees, constantly keeping them focused on the company and on their personal goals.
- Managers will also be kept abreast of constantly changing employment laws, which when understood, reinforced and followed, should help to keep the company out of employee related lawsuits.
- Managers will learn how to effectively balance their time between directing experienced employees and training new employees. This can be a crutch to managers if it is not done correctly.

A common mistake managers often make that contributes to poor employee morale and employee turnover is when managers choose to have only one style of management for all of their employees ranging from the experienced senior level employees to the most inexperienced new hires. This is where the term micro-management probably came from. Unknowingly, the hardworking manager that is "micro-managing" his experienced employees is not intentionally trying to drive away his/her best employees. On the contrary, he/she is just managing everyone the same way, not aware that it is causing resentment among the more experienced employees who feel they do not need to be "told what to do all the time" or "watched all the time". What managers need to realize is that their management style should adjust accordingly based on the level of their employees' experience and expertise in their current position. New employees will need a lot of training and coaching, while experienced employees, thankfully, will just need a bit of coaching, delegating and little training. The best step a new manager can do to help minimize the error of "micro-managing" the wrong employees is to sit down and evaluate their current employees' skill level (size them up) and decide where they fall in relation to their experience level. Then the manager will adjust the management style accordingly. (For more information relevant to this topic, please read Ken Blanchard's and Spencer Johnson's book titled: *The One-Minute Manager.*

EMPLOYEES:

Please be aware that as you grow within an organization your level of experience grows. With that said as you gain more and more experience on the job, naturally your manager should change his style of management from micro-managing to just delegating responsibilities to you. According to the American Management Association, *the sign of a good manager is one who can effectively have a division or an office run smoothly without having to be in the office.* Show your managers you are a reliable and trustworthy employee and assuredly it won't go unnoticed. Ask for tasks to take on when the manager is away at a meeting or on vacation. According to many Fortune 500 Human Resource directors, when companies go to promote from within, they are going to look for the candidate that has the following traits and characteristics: "has always gone above and beyond the scope of the position, was reliable, trustworthy, capable, showed leadership skills, has excellent interpersonal skills and can react well under pressure." Employees should start to invest in their promotability today by asking for extra responsibilities on the job to increase their skills and on the job experiences. The extra investment in yourself that you have commited to by taking on extra tasks on the job, above and beyond your normal job description, will help to develop you as an employee who deserves to be promoted.

As a note: Once you do receive the promotion, don't ever stop assuming extra tasks. *Remember, that was why you received the promotion in the first place.* This commitment to overachievement will continuously help to keep yourself and your career developing in a positive direction.

MANAGERS:

Invest in yourself by attending as many management seminars or classes this year to get an idea as to the management style that fits your company structure, size of employee population, as well as your personality type. Some recommendations are American Management Association and Dale Carnegie Training. If your company does not provide training for management, invest in the training yourself, the rewards will be beneficial to say the least. Try to network with other managers outside of your industry. From a previous chapter, you have already been told of the value of meeting on a monthly or quarterly basis with other managers within the company. Now you need to network outside the company to become aware of other management styles that might enhance productivity and morale in your environment, as well as your interest in still being a manager.

Invest in your employees by investing in your management training. You are their leader. If they don't have a leader that is effective the results will be either employee turnover or negative employee feedback on your leadership skills. You make the choice. Invest in the company and your employees by being the best leader/manager that you can be. No one should be expected to be a top manager without proper training, so invest today by attending the next management sponsored training program, read a new management book or sign yourself up for training outside of work. The rewards will be personally rewarding and your employees will respect you more for being a true professional manager, a leader to emulate.

Lesson 35

Be grateful if you receive bonuses.
If you are in charge of giving out bonuses,
always communicate to your employees
when they should or should not expect them.

YEAR-END BONUSES, quarterly bonuses and performance bonuses are in addition to a person's base salary and can range usually anywhere from 1% to 50% of an employee's base salary. Most companies will base the bonus off the company's year-end profits and will pay the bonus at the end of fourth quarter. Here are a few rules to understand about bonuses.

- Bonuses are not requirements for any company to agree to pay to their employees.
- If your company pays bonuses, be grateful for anything that you receive because there are many companies that never pay out bonuses.
- Not all employees receive bonuses. If you receive a bonus, keep it to yourself. Do not disclose to a co-worker what you received. When this rule is broken and employees disclose what they received to each other there always seems to be one employee who is upset because they found out that someone received more than them.
- In the real world of business, if a company does not make a profit for that year, then that company should probably not be paying out bonuses to anyone. This will and should encourage employees to work harder the next year to help to improve the bottom line.

Every company has a different philosophy as to how they reward their employees. The common thread is that bonuses are a performance incentive for the employee (who is bonus-eligible) throughout the year to accomplish their goals. Most companies will determine who gets what based on their gross margin profits and contribution to the company throughout the year.

Even though bonuses contribute nicely to the bottom line of any employee's salary, employees and managers should never expect a bonus to "keep their head above water" or "the wolves away from the door." Instead, they should manage their money better. This may involve speaking to a financial planner to learn to save more by setting up a 401k plan, Roth IRA or any other tax deferred savings program. A good word of advice if you do receive a year-end bonus, is to start to tell your company to place your bonus in your company 401k plan or other investment accounts pretax. That way, you can maximize the amount that you will receive from the bonus and then just let it grow in an investment account. If you develop this habit early on and discipline yourself to do this with every bonus that you receive, you should end up a financially stable person that will not have to worry about saving money for retirement or for an emergency as long as the stock market does well. When you don't invest the money right away and instead receive the bonus in a hard check form or as a direct deposit, what is guaranteed to occur is that a good percentage of that bonus is going to go to Uncle Sam instead of in your pocket. Another way to avoid jumping into a higher tax bracket because of a year-end bonus, is to request to have the bonus cut in January's payroll to stay in the same tax bracket for the previous year and then adjust your contributions accordingly the next year to keep your taxable income as low as possible.

EMPLOYEES:

Find out what your bonus potential is. Before you accept an offer, talk to previous or current employees of the company to inquire what has been paid out in the past, if possible. As a reminder, always go above and beyond in your job whether you are bonus-eligible or not. Hopefully the company you are working for believes in bonuses. If they don't incentify their employees with cash bonuses, try to encourage them to give back in other ways, such as: company stock, a matching 401k, increased vacation time, gym memberships, company credit cards, clothing allowances, monthly gas allowance cards, or the opportunity to work half days or from home on Fridays, etc. Get creative. Many times the rewards of a non-monetary performance incentive plan is more rewarding and self-gratifying than a year-end bonus that will often be only 2/3 of the cash after Uncle Sam takes his portion (unless you accept my advice of placing it into a tax-deferred account).

MANAGERS:

If the year-end profits are not as good as they have been in the past and bonuses take a huge cut or are eliminated altogether, it is critically important that the manager communicates with each employee to inform them that the bonuses are reduced or eliminated because the profits are down. It is imperative to still enforce with the employees that all of their efforts are appreciated and that you hope they understand why the company cannot pay out the bonus.

Speaking from experience, it is much better to be told that you will not receive a bonus before the anticipated bonus "wait-time" starts (usually from November 26th to December 31st) than to keep waiting for a bonus that never comes. That is absolute torture! No wonder so many people get depressed during the holidays; some of the depression might be because of this "bonus torture" waiting period!

What management must be aware of from this day forward while reading this lesson is: *when a deserving employee is expecting a bonus at the end of the year, that employee will torture themselves in anticipation and disappointment each and every day until they either get their bonus or are finally told that they are not getting their bonus for that year.* During this "bonus-torture" period many negative thoughts occur. The employee starts to build up resentment against the company for not communicating with them about when they will receive their bonus or even just when they will be *told* that they won't receive the bonus. As a result, after weeks of mental torture the employee sometimes starts to look in the classified ads for a better place to work where there is an open dialogue about bonuses. They sometimes start to question the stability of the industry that they work in and will, of course, start to question other employees in the company as to whether they received their bonuses yet. As a result of all of this "bonus torture" the morale goes down and production is affected; all because management did not communicate effectively about whether the bonuses will be paid out or not.

Managers, once again, when bonuses are not paid out due to decreased profits, it is critical that the manager communicates this message to the employees as soon as possible. Management must take the time to inform the employees that they won't unfortunately be receiving bonuses because of a decrease in profits but that their hard work is deeply appreciated. When this is done in a timely manner, the employees should then be able to put closure on the anticipation potential. Ironically, most employees respond well to this communication and in fact usually will work even harder in the coming year to increase profits that will hopefully provide bonuses the next time. I hope this lesson was helpful to any manager who is struggling with this very sensitive issue.

Communication, positive or negative, is the key to happy, dedicated loyal employees.

Life Lesson #8

Don't be a quitter.

NOW THAT YOU HAVE INVESTED in yourself and in your career by reading *Gumption* in its entirety, please go after all that you have set out to accomplish in life. Always keep this book close by to refer to as your career progresses. As you mature you will experience new situations that you might not be prepared for. It is then that I encourage you to read through *Gumption* again, but this time from a different perspective. As your roles and responsibilities change over the course of your career, some of these lessons will serve more value than others depending on what you are relating to at that time. *Gumption* was written to be a resource for a lifetime, not just for a one time review. Coincidentally, the first time you read this book you will probably be an employee and view everything from the employee's perspective. The second time you read this book it will be from a manager's perspective because you would have probably just been promoted because of your strong human relation skills, positive attitude and excellent work habits.

In reference to accomplishing your personal and career goals, please don't allow anyone to stand in your way. Believe in yourself, stay positive and continue to improve every day by investing in yourself. Expect life's obstacles to disappoint you; these hurdles are needed for personal growth and maturity. With every obstacle that you overcome you only increase your wisdom and experience so that you will be able to handle the fame, fortune and added stress that will come along as you accomplish your business and personal goals in life. Good luck, believe in yourself, stay focused, don't be afraid to be passionate and excited about your interests, don't worry about what other people think about you and accomplish everything you set out to do in life! When you stay passionate about what you believe in, then you truly are a success! Create memories not regrets!

I am grateful that you have read *Gumption* and I look forward to writing more books for you to enjoy in the future.

— Lisa Rose

"Things change when you care enough to grab whatever you love (or are passionate about), and give it everything." — Amanda Burr

Gumption
Lesson List

- Please recall that many of the successful business leaders in the market-place today are not any smarter than you or I. They made it to the top because they disciplined themselves by using many of these basic lessons on a daily basis.

- A very wise person once said that 99% of the things that people stress out about never happen. So don't stress out over something that hasn't happened on the job or at home. It is unproductive and a terrible use of your time. If the situation can't be prevented, at least wait until the situation occurs before you start stressing out over it!

- Keep in mind that every person that you meet can teach you something. Be open-minded and listen to the advice of others. Accept what you think is valuable. Acknowledge the rest, don't agree or disagree but be aware of other people's opinions and why they feel that way.

- If you want to make the best first impression with someone, introduce yourself and let that person talk about themselves (thank you, Dale Carnegie).

- Take a risk. Don't regret never taking a chance on something. Make decisions, don't be indecisive.

- Compliments are nice and flattering, but don't overdue the compliments to gain rapport. It can be a turnoff and a deal breaker.

- "Treat every person that you meet, as if they are the most important person in the entire world because to them they are." — unknown

- Don't stress out over daily tasks. If the situation is not life-threatening, please don't let it affect your state of mind. If there is something you can learn from the experience, be grateful because it will make you that much stronger the next time you encounter a similar situation.

- To prevent yourself from added stress in the office, don't get involved in office gossip. If you are engaged in a conversation where gossip is introduced, don't agree to it, add to it or repeat the gossip. Your co-workers will have more respect for you if you stay neutral and you will keep yourself out of trouble.

- Don't quit your favorite job to get out of debt. Instead, get rid of your debt!

- Don't swear or use foul language. The English language has hundreds of thousands of words. Get creative and expressively describe your feelings. Nothing is more of a turnoff than someone who uses vulgarities on a constant basis.

- Learn to respond, not to react!

- Keep everything in moderation. Drink in moderation, if you drink at all. Exercise in moderation, volunteer your time with someone that can benefit from your support, spend time with friends and family, eat in moderation, spend time in nature, go on vacations, enjoy museums and concerts, etc. Simply stated, enjoy the splender of art, friendships, health, nature and love.

- Understand how people learn. Make sure your messages are clear and understood by making your presentations appealing visually, kinesthetically and auditorily. Appeal to their senses not yours.

- Attendance: Don't just call out because you don't feel like working. Consider your co-workers and how it will affect them if you do call out and then decide to go to work if you really don't need to take the time off unexpectedly.

- Have a thirst for knowledge and never stop learning.

- Please don't let others distract you or intimidate you from accomplishing your goal. It is your goal not theirs. Stay focused and keep taking steps toward all of your goals.

- If you don't take action on a career goal, then it is not going to magically appear. Take control of your career before someone else has control over it.

- Stop worrying about what other people think. No one is perfect in this world. Focus on your strengths and enjoy working on your weaknesses, it will make you a stronger person in the long run.

- Don't criticize anyone in a social setting. If you don't have anything nice to say, don't say anything at all.

- Regarding adversity, look forward to obstacles because once you overcome them, you will be that much wiser and stronger than you would have been without them.

- Be grateful for what you have and who you are (health, family, etc.).

- "Happiness is an inside job" (Earl Nightingale); don't expect anything from the outside to make you happy. You are in charge of being happy at all times. Remember your past accomplishment to remind you that you can do anything you set your mind to.

- Help other people. Volunteer your time.

- Understand all situations from both sides (all sides).

- As an employee, show respect to the people who have the authority to fire you on the job. If you disagree with a person in the ranks, talk to them one-on-one. Don't compromise their authority in front of an audience because you may just lose your job.

- Don't make a decision when you are emotionally upset. Take the emotion out of it, cool off by getting a glass of water, stepping outside, etc. Always take the emotion out of making a decision or confronting someone. Don't make rash decisions.

- If you are temporarily confused, be excited. It may mean you are about to learn something but only if you ask the right question and listen to the answer.

- Give examples why rules are in place. It is critical in any industry to enforce a rule or a regulation by making it real and tangible. Relate the policy or rule to the reason why the rule is in effect. Tell the story behind the rule if you know it because there will be a higher chance of retention if the employees/managers understand the consequences of the rule personally.

- Do one or more act of kindness a day.

- Communication is essential in any type of business relationship. Internal communication with co-workers and managers is the lifeline. Without communication production, employee morale and company credibility suffers.

- Managers and employees should not be best friends with their co-workers.

- Constantly look for opportunities to improve and broaden your skills. Keep yourself marketable.

- Do one task at a time and give that task 100% of your attention. When given a task, concentrate 100% on that task while you are completing it. Shut your door if you have to, hold all calls, do what it takes to make sure your best effort is given every time.

- Document changes and keep equal communication between all parties. Don't ever try to memorize everything that is said in a meeting, instead take notes. Always have paper and pen at hand.

- Less is more legally. Don't put anything in writing that can be misinterpreted. Don't put anything in writing that you are unsure of. If you hesitate that the information is incorrect or outdated, don't put it in writing.

- Don't rely on a company to promote you; instead get yourself promoted and choose wisely who you work for.

- Do like things together. Master your time early on in your career to establish a valuable habit that will reward you for a lifetime.

- Know your company goal. If you are in charge of setting your company goal make sure it is clear and attainable to all your employees.

- Set a personal goal for yourself at least once a year and accomplish it!

- Pick your battles. Not every battle has to be fought. Use your judgment as to which complaints are priorities and which can be deferred to a later time.

- Remember that difficult situations, stressors and obstacles are all part of life and business. Learn to deal with them effectively. They are not going to stop coming.

- Don't forget about the basics. As the speed of the business progresses, don't skip the basics or the result could be a loss of a client or worse, your job.

- All employees can and should be managed differently based on their level of competence and experience.

- When the time is right place the blame on company policy to reduce misdirected criticism and undue stress.

- Squealing: should you do it? Answer: put yourself in the owner's shoes and ask yourself the question again.

- Bonuses: appreciate them if you get them. Work hard anyway and if the bonuses are scaled back or eliminated, be sure as a manager or owner in charge of bonuses to communicate with your staff immediately to eliminate "bonus torture".

- Last but not least, don't be a quitter. Give your goal all your effort. Stay focused, believe in yourself and keep taking those ministeps to get you where you want to go no matter how long it takes you!

Thank you for reading *Gumption*.
To place an order for additional copies, please contact:

Gumption Training Company
P.O. Box 17
Monroe, CT 06468
(866) 945-9985

or go online to:
www.gumptiontraining.com

Got Gumption?